# SPECTRUM®

## Common Core Edition

# Language Arts
# and Math

Published by Spectrum®
An imprint of Carson-Dellosa Publishing LLC
Greensboro, North Carolina

Spectrum®
An imprint of Carson-Dellosa Publishing LLC
P.O. Box 35665
Greensboro, NC 27425  USA

ISBN 978-1-4838-0597-9

01-046157811

© Carson-Dellosa • CD-734044

# Table of Contents

Main Ideas and Details • Characters, Settings, and Events • Words that Show Feelings • Fiction and Nonfiction • Point of View • Using Illustrations • Comparing Characters • Reading for Details • Main Ideas • Vocabulary Words • Using a Chart • Using Graphics • Using a Graph • Comparing Texts • Finding Reasons • Complete Sentences • Word Families • Beginning, Middle, and Ending Sounds • Consonant Blends and Digraphs • One-Syllable Words • Multi-Syllable Words • Long Vowel Sounds • Vowel Teams • Compound Words • Verbs • Irregular Words • Writing an Opinion • Writing to Inform • Writing a Story • Journal Writing • Revising • Using Digital Tools • Research • Nouns • Letters and Words • Adjectives • Conjunctions • Articles • Prepositions • Types of Sentences • Pronouns • Commas • Prefixes and Suffixes • Categories • Shades of Meaning • Words from Reading

Equations • Addition • Subtraction • Word Problems • Number Families • Subtraction Strategies • Addition Strategies • Addition and Subtraction • Numbers and Number Words • Numbers and Counting • Place Value • Comparing Numbers • Adding Two-Digit Numbers • Subtracting Two-Digit Numbers • Adding and Subtracting 10 • Addition with Regrouping • Comparing Lengths • Measuring with Units • Measurement Problems • Telling Time • Counting Data • Shapes • Composite Shapes • Equal Parts • Halves • Fourths • Fourths and Halves

# Introduction to the Common Core State Standards
## Grade 1

**Why Are Common Core State Standards Important for My Child?**

The Common Core State Standards are a set of guidelines that outline what children are expected to learn at school. Most U.S. states have voluntarily adopted the standards. Teachers, principals, and administrators in these states use the standards as a blueprint for classroom lessons, district curriculum, and statewide tests. The standards were developed by a state-led collaboration between the Council of Chief State School Officers (CCSSO) and the National Governors Association (NGA).

The Common Core Standards set high expectations for your child's learning. They are up-to-date with 21st century technology and draw on the best practices of excellent schools around the world. They focus on important skills in reading, language arts, and math. Common Core State Standards aim to ensure that your child will be college and career ready by the end of high school and able to compete in our global world.

© Carson-Dellosa • CD-734044

## What Are the Common Core State Standards for My First Grade Student?

Common Core State Standards for your first grader are designed to build a solid foundation for reading, literacy, and mathematical understanding. On practice pages in this book, you will find references to specific Common Core Standards that teachers will expect your child to know by the end of the year. Completing activities on these pages will help your child master essential skills for success in first grade.

### A Sample of Common Core Language Arts Skills for Grade 1*

- Explain differences between fictional books and books that provide factual information.
- Read two stories, then compare and contrast the experiences of the two main characters.
- Use tables of contents, headings, glossaries, electronic menus, and other features to find information in texts.
- Think about the reasons an author gives to back up points.
- Pick out the beginning, middle, and ending sounds in one-syllable words.
- Write to give opinions, provide information, and tell stories.
- Use conjunctions such as *and*, *but*, and *or* to join two sentences.
- Choose the right verb to use in a sentence: *He walks*; *we walk*.

### A Sample of Common Core Math Skills for Grade 1*

- Use addition and subtraction within 20 to solve word problems.
- Know that since *8 + 3 = 11*, then *3 + 8 = 11* is also true.
- Count to 120, starting with any number.
- Put three objects in order by length.
- Tell time in hours and half-hours.
- Make larger shapes from smaller shapes.
- Divide circles and rectangles into halves and fourths.

### How to Use This Book

In this book, you will find a complete **Common Core State Standards Overview** for first grade English Language Arts (pages 6–9) and Math (pages 64–67). Read these pages to learn more about the Common Core Standards and what you can expect your child to learn at school this year.

Then, choose **Practice Pages** that best address your child's needs for building skills that meet specific standards. Help your child complete practice pages and check the answers.

Finally, assist your child in cutting apart the **Flash Cards** found at the back of the book. These handy cards, which provide even more practice with Common Core skills, are suitable for use at home or on the go.

 At the bottom of each practice page, you will find a **Helping at Home** tip that provides fun and creative ideas for additional practice with the skill at home.

# Common Core State Standards for English Language Arts*

The following parent-friendly explanations of first grade Common Core English language arts standards are provided to help you understand what your child will learn in school this year. Practice pages listed will help your child master each skill.

Complete Common Core State Standards may be found here: www.corestandards.org.

## RL/RI.1 Reading Standards for Literature and Informational Text

### Key Ideas and Details
### (Standards: RL.1.1, RL.1.2, RL.1.3, RI.1.1, RI.1.2, RI.1.3)

*After reading a story or information article, your child will ask and answer questions about details from the text.* • **Practice pages: 10, 11, 15, 18**

*After reading a story, your child will describe the message or lesson of the story. After reading an information article, your child will describe its main topic.* • **Practice pages: 10, 11, 15, 19**

*After reading a story, your child will describe its characters, settings, and major events.* • **Practice pages: 12, 15, 16**

*After reading a nonfiction article, your child will make connections between pieces of information discussed in the text.* • **Practice page: 21**

### Craft and Structure
### (Standards: RL.1.4, RL.1.5, RL.1.6, RI.1.4, RI.1.5, RI.1.6)

*After reading a story or poem, your child will point out words and phrases that suggest feelings or appeal to the senses.* • **Practice page: 13**

*When your child comes to an unknown word, he or she will ask questions to find out its meaning.* • **Practice page: 20**

*Your child will learn the difference between fictional books that tell stories and nonfiction books that provide information.* • **Practice page: 14**

*Your child will learn the habit of using text features such as boldface words, headings, tables of contents, and glossaries to find information.* • **Practice pages: 18–21, 23**

*Your child will think about point of view and decide who is telling the story.* • **Practice page: 15**

When reading nonfiction articles, your child will look for information provided by illustrations and graphics as well as text. • **Practice pages: 21, 22, 23**

### Integration of Knowledge and Skills
### (Standards: RL.1.7, RL.1.9, RI.1.7, RI.1.8, RI.1.9)

When reading, your child will use illustrations and graphics as well as details from the text to describe key ideas, characters, settings, and events. • **Practice pages: 16, 22, 23**

When reading a nonfiction article, your child will look for reasons and evidence an author uses to back up points. • **Practice page: 26**

Your child will compare and contrast the experiences of different characters in stories or compare and contrast two nonfiction articles about the same topic. • **Practice pages: 17, 24, 25**

## RF.1 Reading Standards: Foundational Skills

### Print Concepts
### (Standard: RF.1.1a)

Your child will learn that a sentence always begins with a capital letter and always ends with a punctuation mark. • **Practice pages: 27, 55, 56**

### Phonological Awareness
### (Standards: RF.1.2a, RF.1.2b, RF.1.2c, RF.1.2d)

Your child will listen to words and tell whether they hear a short vowel sound (as in cap) or a long vowel sound (as in cape). • **Practice pages: 28, 31**

Your child will listen for each sound in a word and blend sounds together to make words. For a word such as map, your child will identify the beginning sound (/m/), the middle sound (short a), and the ending sound (/p/). • **Practice pages: 29, 30, 31**

### Phonics and Word Recognition
### (Standards: RF.1.3a, RF.1.3b, RF.1.3c, RF.1.3d, RF.1.3e, RF.1.3f, RF.1.3g)

Your child will learn that in some words, two consonants blend together to make a single sound (for example, sl in sled). • **Practice page: 32**

Your child will learn that long vowel sounds are spelled in many ways. In words like cube, the vowel sound is spelled vowel-consonant-silent e. In words like boat, wait, coin, and feet, the vowel sound is spelled with vowel combinations or "vowel teams." • **Practice pages: 35, 36**

# Common Core State Standards for English Language Arts*

*Your child will read multi-syllable words by breaking them into syllables. Each syllable contains a vowel sound.* • **Practice pages: 33, 34, 37**

*Your child will understand that prefixes such as re– (as in redo) and suffixes such as –ing (as in walking) can be added to words.* • **Practice pages: 38, 39, 58**

*Your child will learn that some words are not spelled like they sound. He or she will learn to spell words with irregular spellings such as they and your.* • **Practice page: 40**

## W.1 Writing Standards

### Text Types and Purposes
### (Standards: W.1.1, W.1.2, W.1.3)

*Your child will state an opinion in writing and give a reason to support the opinion.* • **Practice pages: 41, 42**

*Your child will write to provide facts about a topic.* • **Practice pages: 42, 46, 47**

*Your child will write stories that include two or more events and details about what happens in the story.* • **Practice pages: 43, 44, 45, 46, 48**

### Production and Distribution of Writing
### (Standards: W.1.5, W.1.6)

*Your child will revise writing to make it more interesting and to answer questions from readers.* • **Practice page: 45**

*Your child will write on a computer and print out his or her work to share with others.* • **Practice page: 46**

### Research to Build and Present Knowledge
### (Standards: W.1.7, W.1.8)

*Your child will gather ideas for writing by researching and by thinking about his or her own experiences.* • **Practice pages: 43, 47, 48**

## L.1 Language Standards

### Conventions of Standard English
### (Standards: L.1.1a, L.1.1b, L.1.1c, L.1.1d, L.1.1e, L.1.1f, L.1.1g, L.1.1h, L.1.1i, L.1.1j, L.1.2a, L.1.2b, L.1.2c)

Your child will practice writing all 26 alphabet letters in both uppercase and lowercase forms.
• **Practice page: 50**

Your child will learn that common nouns such as dog and chair begin with lowercase letters and proper nouns such as Mario and Elm Street begin with capital letters. • **Practice page: 49**

Your child will learn to make subjects and verbs agree in sentences such as He walks and They walk. He or she will use verbs in the past, present, and future tense.
• **Practice pages: 38, 39, 50**

Your child will learn to add variety to writing by sometimes replacing the names of people and things with pronouns such as he, she, and it. • **Practice page: 56**

Your child will use adjectives such as blue and soft to describe things. • **Practice page: 51**

Your child will use words such as and, but, and or to join two related sentences. The sentences I like to swim and I like to dive can be combined: I like to swim and dive. • **Practice page: 52**

Your child will use the articles a or an in front of a word depending on its beginning sound: a grape, an orange. • **Practice page: 53**

Your child will use prepositions such as beyond and toward to explain where things are located or how they relate to each other. • **Practice page: 54**

Your child will read and write sentences that end with periods, question marks, and exclamation marks. • **Practice pages: 55, 56**

Your child will learn to use capital letters and commas in names such as James Hall, dates such as January 12, 2018, and lists such as yellow, green, and blue. • **Practice pages: 49, 57**

### Vocabulary Acquisition and Use
### (Standards: L.1.4b, L.1.4c, L.1.5a, L.1.5b, L.1.5d, L.1.6)

Your child will understand that prefixes such as re– (as in redo) and suffixes such as –ing (as in walking) can change the meanings of words. • **Practice pages: 38, 39, 58**

Your child will sort items into logical categories. For example, he or she will sort foods into fruits and vegetables. • **Practice pages: 59–61**

Your child will think about differences between words that have similar meanings, such as walk, march, and strut. • **Practice page: 62**

Your child will learn new words from reading and use them in speaking and writing.
• **Practice page: 63**

# Main Ideas and Details

Read the story. Answer the questions.

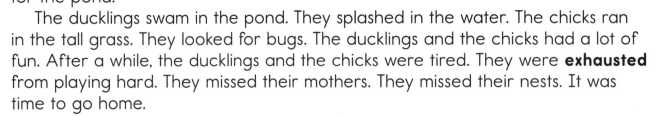

## At the Pond

One warm spring day, the ducklings decided to go to the pond. The ducklings wanted to go for a swim.

"Can we go too?" the chicks asked.

"Chicks cannot swim," the ducklings laughed.

"We will run in the tall grass and look for bugs. Please let us come."

So, the ducklings and the chicks set off for the pond.

The ducklings swam in the pond. They splashed in the water. The chicks ran in the tall grass. They looked for bugs. The ducklings and the chicks had a lot of fun. After a while, the ducklings and the chicks were tired. They were **exhausted** from playing hard. They missed their mothers. They missed their nests. It was time to go home.

1. The main idea is the big point of the story. Which sentence tells the main idea?
   A. Ducklings have fun swimming.
   B. Chicks and ducklings hatch from eggs.
   C. Both ducklings and chicks can have fun at the pond.

2. A detail is a small point in the story. Which sentence tells a detail?
   A. They looked for bugs.
   B. Both ducklings and chicks can have fun at the pond.
   C. A flower grew by the pond.

3. What does the word *exhausted* mean?
   A. tired
   B. silly
   C. angry

Helping at Home

Talk about your child's favorite movie or TV show. Make a statement about it such as "the boat had a leak," or "the boy was happy because he made new friends." Ask your child to tell whether each statement is a detail or a main idea.

# Main Ideas and Details

Read the story. Answer the questions.

## The Fox and His Trap

One day, Fox was busy making something. Turtle came by.

"What are you making, Fox?" Turtle asked. "Nothing," Fox answered. "It looks like a trap to me," Turtle said as he walked away.

Soon, Mouse came by. "What are you making, Fox?" Mouse asked. "Nothing," Fox answered. "It looks like a trap to me," Mouse said as he crawled away.

Before long, Duck came by. "What are you making, Fox?" Duck asked. "Nothing," Fox answered. "It looks like a trap to me," Duck said as she waddled away.

Just as Fox finished, Rabbit came by. "What did you make, Fox?" Rabbit asked. "A home for a rabbit," Fox said. "It looks like a trap to me," Rabbit said. "Nonsense," Fox said. "Come closer and have a look."

"But I don't think I will fit," Rabbit said.

"Nonsense!" Fox laughed. "It's big enough for me." Fox crawled inside. With Fox inside, Rabbit shut the latch. The door was shut tight. Rabbit hopped off, saying, "It looks like a trap to me."

1. Who got caught in Fox's trap?
   A. the turtle
   B. the mouse
   C. the fox

2. Why did Fox want to make a trap?
   A. He liked to build things.
   B. He wanted to catch Rabbit.
   C. He had extra wood.

3. Why do you think the fox always said, "Nothing," when others asked what he was making? _____

4. Why do you think Rabbit knew to shut the latch? _____

**Helping at Home**

When your child tells you a real or made-up story, ask three questions about the story's details or main ideas. Invite your child to tell the story again, this time including answers to your questions.

# Characters, Settings, and Events

Read the story. Answer the questions.

## A Hot Summer Day

It was a hot summer day. "This is a good day to be lazy. I will lie in the shade of the apple tree," Billy said.

Soon, Katie came skipping by. "What are you doing?" she asked.

"Oh, nothing," Billy replied.

"I think I will do nothing, too," Katie said. She sat down next to Billy.

They saw an ant pulling a big leaf. A ladybug flew onto Katie's hand. A grasshopper hopped by. A bee landed on a flower. "It is fun doing nothing," Billy and Katie said.

1. Write a sentence to tell the main event of the story. _____

_____

| Draw the setting. It is where the story takes place. | Draw Billy and Katie. |
| --- | --- |
| | |

© Carson-Dellosa • CD-734044

# Words that Show Feelings

Read the poem.

I
love
spring
more than
anything.
More than anything,
I love spring.

I like to sing in the spring
about the flowers spring brings
and how I wish
I were a bird with wings.

I like to hold a kite
by its string
and fly on a swing.
I feel like a king
in the
spring.

Answer the questions.

1. Find a word or a group of words in the poem that shows feeling. Write it on

   the line. _____

2. Write a sentence about the word or the group of words you wrote. _____

   _____

3. Have you ever felt this way? Write a sentence about it. _____

   _____

**Helping at Home**

Choose summer, winter, or fall. Brainstorm with your child a list of words that describe the season. Talk about what feelings the words evoke. You may wish to use the words to write sentences or a poem.

# Fiction and Nonfiction

Some books tell stories. They are called **fiction**. Some books give facts. They are called **nonfiction**.

Read the titles. Check what kind of book it is.

| Book Title | Story (Fiction) | Fact (Nonfiction) |
|---|---|---|
| 1. *The Life of the President* | | |
| 2. *Natalie's Great Clubhouse in Her Yard* | | |
| 3. *How to Peddle a Bike* | | |
| 4. *The History of the State of Texas* | | |
| 5. *Mike's Field Trip to the Zoo* | | |

Find three books. Write down the titles. Check what kind of book it is.

| Book Title | Story (Fiction) | Fact (Nonfiction) |
|---|---|---|
| 6. | | |
| 7. | | |
| 8. | | |

**Helping at Home**

Visit a public library with your child. Choose one of your child's favorite subjects, such as pets or trains. Ask a librarian to help your child locate both fiction and nonfiction books about the subject. Read and compare the two types of books.

# Point of View

Read the story. Answer the questions.

## The Race

Sammy Snail was sad. He wanted to run in the big race, but he was too slow. Robby Rabbit hopped up to Sammy Snail. "Why are you so sad?" he asked.

"I am too slow to be in the big race," Sammy Snail cried.

"Sammy Snail, you are too slow!" Robby Rabbit laughed as he hopped down the road.

Kami Kangaroo saw Sammy Snail on her way to the race. "Why are you crying?" she asked.

"I am too slow to be in the big race," cried Sammy Snail.

"Don't cry. I will help you," Kami Kangaroo. said. She picked up Sammy Snail. She dropped him in her kangaroo pouch.

Soon, it was time for the big race. Robby Rabbit and Kami Kangaroo raced together. As they hopped to the finish line, Kami Kangaroo took Sammy Snail out of her pouch. She set him down across the finish line. Sammy Snail won the big race!

1. Who are the characters in this story? _____

2. Which animal told Sammy Snail he was too slow? _____

3. Which animal helped Sammy Snail? _____

4. A narrator tells a story but is not a character in the story. This story has a narrator. Write a sentence from the narrator's part of the text. _____

_____

**Helping at Home**

Together with your child, make up a simple story that takes place on a school playground. Then, have fun retelling the story from the point of view of different characters and onlookers: an older child, a younger child, a teacher, an ant, etc.

# Using Illustrations

Read the story. Answer the questions.

## The Show

Ruby and her friends put on a music show. The show was in July. Judy played a tune on her flute. Hugo played the bugle. Luke marched in his new uniform. Susan danced in her cute tutu. June and Ruby played a duet on their lutes. Duke played his huge tuba to end the show. Ruby said her friends were all super!

1. Color the picture. Look at the people in the picture.

2. Who did you color? _____

3. Who are the characters? _____

4. What is the setting, or where the story takes place? _____

5. What was the main event? _____

_____

**Helping at Home**

Do an online search for an image of a famous painting such as van Gogh's *Starry Night* or Chagall's *I and the Village*. Admire the pictures with your child, pointing out and describing details. Invite your child to make up stories about the paintings.

## Comparing Characters

Read the story.

### A Tale of Two Mice

Once upon a time, two little mice lived happily. One mouse lived under a vine outside a large house. The other mouse lived under the tiles inside the large house.

The vine mouse liked to eat plain rice. The tile mouse liked to eat bites of fine food.

The vine mouse liked to play hide-and-seek outside. The tile mouse liked to sit inside.

The two mice were opposites. Still, the two mice were fine friends.

Fill in the chart. Write three facts about the vine mouse and the tile mouse.

| Vine Mouse | Tile Mouse |
| --- | --- |
|  |  |

# Reading for Details

Butterflies are lovely to look at, but here is how to make one you can eat!

## Tasty Butterflies

You will need:

- 2 frozen pancakes
- 1 banana
- 2 grapes
- 2 pieces of link sausage
- 2 toothpicks
- jelly

Here is how to make it:

- Toast the pancakes and cut them in half. This will make the four pieces you will need for the four wings of the butterfly.
- Peel the banana and place it on the plate. This will be the butterfly's body.
- Place the cut sides of the pancakes next to the banana to form the butterfly's wings.
- Spread jelly on the "wings."
- Use the toothpicks to hold the grapes on the banana as eyes.
- Cook the sausages and place them at the top of the banana as antennae.

Use details from the text to fill in the missing words.

1. The _____ will make the butterfly's body.

2. The wings will be covered with _____.

3. Butterflies have four _____.

4. The antennae will be made from _____.

5. A butterfly has two _____ to see with.

Use a cereal box or other product package. Challenge your child to answer your questions based on text he or she can find on the package. Ask, "What is in the box? How much does it weigh? What is it made of? How do you use it?"

Helping at Home

# Main Ideas

Each title tells a main idea. Write each title above the correct passage. Remember to ask yourself, "Does this title tell about the whole passage?"

The Water Cycle of the Dead Sea

What is the Dead Sea?

The Uses of the Dead Sea

The Salty Waters of the Dead Sea

1. _____

_____

The Dead Sea is a saltwater lake. It is in Asia. It is near Jordan and Israel. The lake is very deep. It is deeper at the north end. It is over 1000 feet below sea level. The south end of the Dead Sea is shallow.

2. _____

_____

The Dead Sea is much saltier than the ocean! The salt is very thick. No plants can grow in the water. No animals can live in the water. That is why it is called the Dead Sea. The salt is so thick that swimmers can float on top!

3. _____

_____

The Dead Sea is valuable. It is easy to get salt from it. People use the water for beauty and health. Some people go there to fix skin problems. Many people go to the Dead Sea for those reasons.

4. _____

_____

The Dead Sea gets water from the Jordan River. The river goes into the sea. Other small streams go into the Dead Sea, too. No rivers lead out of the sea. The water stays in place. It gets very salty this way. The Dead Sea is in a desert, so it gets salty fast!

Helping at Home

Look at a nonfiction book or Web site with your child. Read some headings and subheadings aloud. Ask your child to make predictions about what facts will be found below. Read on to find out if your child's guesses are correct.

# Vocabulary Words

Read the text. Look at the bold words closely.

## Hamsters

Hamsters are small animals. They were found in Syria hundreds of years ago. They live in many parts of the world. Hamsters like to **hoard**, or keep, food in their big cheeks. Their cheeks are like pouches. They store nuts and seeds inside. Hamsters are known to like to stay up at night. This means they are **nocturnal**. Some family members think hamsters are great pets. But hamsters like to **stay up very late**!

Answer the questions.

1. What does the word *hoard* mean? _____

_____

2. What does the word *nocturnal* mean? _____

_____

3. What does it mean to stay up very late? _____

_____

4. Choose a bold word or group of words. Write your own sentence using the

word or group of words. _____

_____

Let your child decorate a craft stick with question marks and a pair of eyes. When reading together, let your child point the stick at unknown words. Then, search the surrounding words for clues to the new word's meaning.

# Using a Chart

Charts and tables are helpful in organizing information. To read the chart, match the given information from the top and the left side to find new information in the boxes.

| | Monday | Tuesday | Wednesday | Thursday | Friday |
|---|---|---|---|---|---|
| **Reading** | Sandie | Elena | Sam | Kendra | Evan |
| **Listening** | Elena | Sam | Kendra | Evan | Sandie |
| **Math** | Sam | Kendra | Evan | Sandie | Elena |
| **Art** | Kendra | Evan | Sandie | Elena | Sam |
| **Science** | Evan | Sandie | Elena | Sam | Kendra |

Use the chart to answer the questions.

1. Who will use the art center on Thursday? _____

2. What center will Sam use on Monday? _____

3. On what day will Evan use the science center? _____

4. What center will Sandie use on Friday? _____

5. Who will use the reading center on Wednesday? _____

6. On what day will Elena use the math center? _____

**Helping at Home**

Help your child make a silly chart that shows what kind of candy he or she would like to eat for breakfast, lunch, and dinner for one week. Have your child ask you questions based on the information in the chart.

# Using Graphics

Look at the pictures. What do you see? Write a fact under each one.

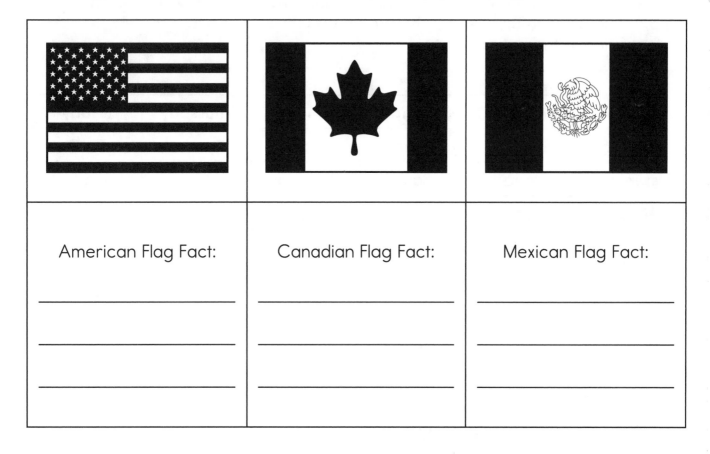

| American Flag Fact: | Canadian Flag Fact: | Mexican Flag Fact: |
|---|---|---|
| _____ | _____ | _____ |
| _____ | _____ | _____ |
| _____ | _____ | _____ |

The pictures give information. We can tell what the flags look like from the pictures. Read the flag facts below. Underline the color words.

| The American flag has stripes. It is red, white, and blue. The American flag has stars. | The Canadian flag has a maple leaf. It is red and white. The leaf is red. | The Mexican flag has a bird. It is red, white, and green. The bird holds a snake. |
|---|---|---|

Helping at Home

Search online for pictures of flags from other nations. Print the pictures and cut them out. Write a sentence about each flag on a card or a slip of paper. Can your child match the pictures and the sentences?

# Using a Graph

Graphs show information. We can compare more than one thing. A bar graph has bars or columns to show information.

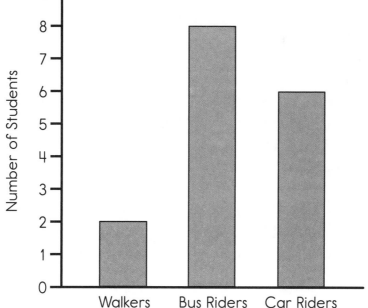

**Mrs. Lopez's First-Grade Class: Ways to Get Home**

Use the bar graph to answer the questions.

1. How many students ride the bus home? _____

2. How many students walk home? _____

3. What is the title of the graph? _____

_____

4. Do more students take the bus or ride in a car? _____

**Helping at Home**

Help your child list facts about the graph above. Include how many children use each mode of transportation, how many children are in the class, etc. Can your child list 10 facts? Read the list together, verifying each fact against the graph.

# Comparing Texts

Read the two passages. Fill in the chart on page 25.

### The Man Who Never Lied
### (An African Tale)

Once, long ago, a man named Mamad lived far away. He never told a lie. All of the people knew he was truthful. The king wanted to meet Mamad. "Mamad, will you ever tell a lie?" the king asked. "No, I will never tell a lie," Mamad said.

A few days later, the king called for Mamad again. He was ready to go hunting. "Mamad, will you tell the queen that I will join her for lunch this afternoon? Please tell her to cook a lot of food," the king said. "Yes, sir," Mamad said. Mamad left. The king laughed and decided not to go hunting and not to leave at all. He wanted Mamad to lie.

Mamad went to the queen. He was smart and said, "Queen, maybe you should make food for your king this afternoon. Maybe you should not. Maybe he will come this afternoon. But maybe not." The queen was confused!

The king told the people Mamad had lied to the queen. Then, the queen told them what Mamad said. The king knew Mamad was a wise man after that.

Mamad never told a lie.

### Pinocchio
### (An Italian Tale)

Many years ago, a man named Geppetto lived in a cottage. He wanted a son. He carved a boy out of wood. The puppet came to life!

Pinocchio the puppet ran away, but he soon came home. Geppetto took care of him and made him food. Geppetto asked where he had been. Pinocchio said he had gone to the park. His nose started to grow! Geppetto knew he was telling a lie. He told him not to do that.

Pinocchio went to school with kids. On his way, he heard music from a puppet show. He told his friends he would be at school soon. His nose started to grow again! He had told a lie. He joined the show and did not go to school.

The puppet master wanted to keep Pinocchio. He told the master he was going to get something. His nose started to grow! He had told a lie again. Pinocchio climbed a tree and started to go home.

Geppetto was worried. He looked for Pinocchio everywhere! He found him and asked where he had been. Pinocchio told Geppetto the whole story. His nose went back to normal. He had learned not to lie.

# Comparing Texts

The tale of Mamad and the tale of Pinocchio are two very similar but different stories. Fill in the chart.

| What was similar between Mamad and Pinocchio? | What was different about Mamad and Pinocchio? |
|---|---|
| _____ _____ _____ _____ _____ _____ _____ | _____ _____ _____ _____ _____ _____ _____ |

1. What did the king learn from Mamad? _____

_____

2. What did Pinocchio learn from Geppetto? _____

_____

3. How do you feel about people who tell lies? _____

_____

**Helping at Home**

Ask your child to recall two events, such as two birthday parties, play dates, or outings. What was similar about the two times? What was different? Ask your child to draw a picture and write a sentence about each event.

# Finding Reasons

Read the text. Answer the question.

Ice cream is the greatest dessert. I like to eat it after dinner. Sometimes, I eat one scoop. Other times, I have two scoops! I like to have chocolate ice cream. I also like mint chocolate chip ice cream. I like ice cream because it is sweet. I like ice cream because it cools me down on a hot day. When I go to the beach, I eat this cold treat!

1. The author is the writer. The author likes ice cream. What two reasons did the author give?

_____

_____

Read the text. Answer the question.

Sand castles are made of sand. I can build them at the beach. I can stack the sand castle up high. I mix water with the sand to help it stay together. I like sand castles because they are fun to build at the beach. I also like them because I can build them with friends. Sand castles are fun to build!

2. The author is the writer. The author likes sand castles. What two reasons did the author give?

_____

_____

**Helping at Home**

When your family must make a decision about what to eat, where to go, etc., invite your child to play reporter and interview each family member to find out his or her opinion and three supporting reasons.

# Complete Sentences

The first word of a sentence begins with an uppercase letter.

**Example:** <u>S</u>ome birds are different.

Write *yes* if the sentence is written correctly. Write *no* if it is not.

1. _____ What is a kea?

2. _____ a kea is a bird.

3. _____ It is a kind of parrot.

4. _____ where do keas live?

5. _____ They live in New Zealand.

6. _____ they are green.

7. _____ keas eat bugs and fruit.

8. Choose a sentence above that was not written correctly. Write it correctly on the lines.

_____

_____

_____

_____

 *Helping at Home*

Choose any two sentences and write each word on an index card. For each sentence, include a card with a capital letter for the first word and one with a punctuation mark for the end. Can your child use the cards to assemble complete sentences?

# Word Families

When words have the same ending sounds and rhyme, these words belong in the same **word family**.

**Examples:** b<u>and</u>, h<u>and</u>, l<u>and</u>

Read each word. Look at the underlined word ending. Then, write as many words as you can for each word family

| r<u>at</u> | T<u>im</u> | k<u>it</u> |
|---|---|---|
| | | |
| r<u>ate</u> | t<u>ime</u> | k<u>ite</u> |
| | | |

**Helping at Home**
Ask your child to pronounce the words he or she wrote above and tell which have short vowel sounds and which have long vowel sounds. Choose several rhyming words and use them to write a silly poem together.

# Beginning, Middle, and Ending Sounds

The words below have a beginning sound, a middle sound, and an ending sound. Say the words aloud. Break the words apart by sound. Place each sound in the box next to the word.

| Word | Beginning Sound | Middle Sound | Ending Sound |
|------|-----------------|--------------|--------------|
| bun  |                 |              |              |
| hip  |                 |              |              |
| get  |                 |              |              |
| sun  |                 |              |              |
| bat  |                 |              |              |

Some words start with two consonants. Consonant blends have two consonants, and each makes one sound.

**Example:** *sw* in swim

Say the words aloud. Break the words apart by sound. Place each sound in the box next to the word. Remember, blends count as two sounds!

| Blend Word | Beginning Blend Sound 1 | Beginning Blend Sound 2 | Middle Sound | Ending Sound |
|------------|-------------------------|-------------------------|--------------|--------------|
| flip       |                         |                         |              |              |
| brim       |                         |                         |              |              |
| swap       |                         |                         |              |              |
| slim       |                         |                         |              |              |
| grip       |                         |                         |              |              |

Helping at Home

Play with magnetic letters or letter tiles from a word game. Give six to each player. Who can use the tiles to spell, blend, and say a word the fastest? Players who cannot make a word may draw another letter from a bag.

# Beginning, Middle, and Ending Sounds

Answer the questions. Be sure to say each word aloud. Listen to each sound as you say the word. Think of what letter stands for each sound.

1. What is the first sound in the word *fish*? _____

2. What is the second sound in the word *hot*? _____

3. What is the last sound in the word *goat*? _____

4. What is the first sound in the word *went*? _____

5. What is the second sound in the word *yes*? _____

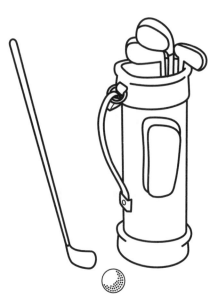

6. What is the last sound in the word *dad*? _____

7. What is the first sound in the word *golf*? _____

8. What is the second sound in the word *fan*? _____

9. What is the last sound in the word *sat*? _____

10. What is the first sound in the word *kite*? _____

11. Say your name aloud. What is the first sound? _____

© Carson-Dellosa • CD-734044

# Beginning, Middle, and Ending Sounds

Each word below has one syllable. Each word has a beginning sound, a middle sound, and an ending sound. The middle sound is a vowel sound. Write the correct sound on the line. A letter stands for a sound.

| | | |
|---|---|---|
| **Beginning Sound** | 1. ___og | 2. ___an |
| | 3. ___op | 4. ___en |
| **Middle Sound** | 5. c___t | 6. j___g |
| | 7. c___p | 8. j___t |
| **Ending Sound** | 9. lo___ | 10. ne___ |
| | 11. ca___ | 12. ba___ |

**Helping at Home**

After your child completes the activity, say the three sounds separately that make up one of the words on the page. For cat, say /c/, /ă/, /t/. Can your child say and point to the word based on your sound clues? Have your child give you clues, too.

# Consonant Blends and Digraphs

**Consonant blends** are two consonant letters next to each other at the beginning or the end of a word. Each letter makes its own sound.

**Examples:** *sn* in <u>sn</u>eeze, *tr* in <u>tr</u>ip, *sl* in <u>sl</u>ow, *cl* in <u>cl</u>own

**Consonant digraphs** are two consonant letters next to each other at the beginning or the end of a word. Together, both letters make one sound.

**Examples:** *sh* in <u>sh</u>ip, *ch* in pit<u>ch</u>, *ck* in so<u>ck</u>, *th* in <u>th</u>in

Decide what consonant blend is missing in each word and write the letters on the lines.

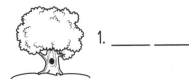 1. ____ ____ee

 2. ____ ____ed

 3. ____ ____oud

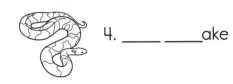 4. ____ ____ake

Decide what consonant digraph is missing in each word and write the letters on the lines.

 5. cat ____ ____

 6. ____ ____ip

 7. wi ____ ____

 8. ____ ____umb

**Helping at Home**

Write these letter pairs on cards or slips of paper and put them in a bag: *bl, br, ch, fl, gr, pl, sh, sm, th, wh.* Can your child draw one and say a word that includes that blend or digraph? You may wish to keep a list of the words named.

# One-Syllable Words

Each syllable in a word has one vowel sound. Use the word families to make one-syllable words. You may use each word family more than once. Do not repeat any words.

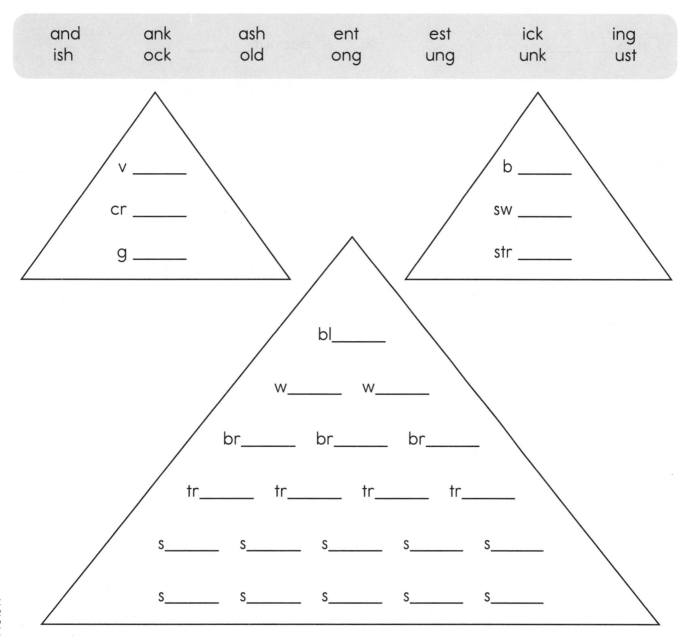

| and | ank | ash | ent | est | ick | ing |
| ish | ock | old | ong | ung | unk | ust |

v _____

cr _____

g _____

b _____

sw _____

str _____

bl_____

w_____ w_____

br_____ br_____ br_____

tr_____ tr_____ tr_____ tr_____

s_____ s_____ s_____ s_____ s_____

s_____ s_____ s_____ s_____ s_____

**Helping at Home**

Help your child make a list of the names of his or her classmates and friends. Say each name. Underline the letters that make each vowel sound. How many syllables does each name have? Do the number of syllables and vowel sounds match?

# Multi-Syllable Words

Find out how many syllables are in each word. Say each word. Count the number of vowels you hear. Write the number on the line.

1. dragon _____

2. frog _____

3. itch _____

4. peanut _____

5. potato _____

6. watermelon _____

7. camera _____

8. hero _____

9. Tyrannosaurus _____

10. journal _____

Look at the words in the word bank. Answer the questions.

| hippopotamus | starfish | tarantula | yard |

11. Which word has five syllables? _____

12. How many syllables does *starfish* have? _____

13. Which word has only one syllable? _____

14. How many syllables does *tarantula* have? _____

*Helping at Home*

Say a one-syllable word, such as *class*. Have your child say a two-syllable word, such as *classroom*. Then, say a three-syllable word. How high can you go? Help your child write the last word given, underlining letters that make the vowel sounds.

# Long Vowel Sounds

When a letter sounds like its name, it makes a long vowel sound.

**Examples:** *a* in l<u>a</u>ke, *i* in h<u>i</u>ke

When a word has a consonant-vowel-consonant-*e* pattern (CVCe), the vowel sound is usually long, and the *e* is silent.

**Examples:** nam<u>e</u>, rid<u>e</u>, not<u>e</u>, cut<u>e</u>

Complete the word at the end of each sentence. Then, find and circle each answer in the word search. Words appear down, diagonally, or backward.

1. A gorilla is a kind of a____ ___.

2. A dog likes to chew on a b____ ____ ____.

3. On a windy day, you can fly a k____ ____ ____.

4. People laugh when they are told a funny j____ ____ ____.

5. You squeeze toothpaste out of a t____ ____ ____.

6. Food is served on a p____ ____ ____ ____.

7. If you are not afraid, you are b____ ____ ____ ____.

8. If you win a game, you sometimes get a p____ ____ ____ ____.

| r | w | p | e | m | l | f | q | e | r |
|---|---|---|---|---|---|---|---|---|---|
| q | g | n | p | g | o | l | r | e | z |
| f | o | j | r | v | a | c | b | p | p |
| b | j | o | i | q | t | u | h | l | e |
| d | g | k | z | i | t | u | a | a | j |
| s | t | e | e | j | b | o | b | t | e |
| j | b | m | i | p | r | c | z | e | k |
| c | a | j | n | r | a | u | q | s | i |
| h | x | p | g | e | v | b | j | d | t |
| u | k | g | e | y | e | e | s | o | e |

Helping at Home

Write *e* on a special sticker or on a star shape cut from paper. Have your child write three-letter words such as *cap*, *fin*, and *cut*, then add the super silent *e* to the end to make new words with long vowel sounds.

# Vowel Teams

**Vowel teams** are two vowel letters next to each other that usually make one sound. The vowel teams *ai*, *ea*, *ee*, and *oa* often make a long vowel sound.

**Examples:** w<u>ai</u>t, r<u>ea</u>l, b<u>ee</u>, g<u>oa</u>t

Read each clue. Then, complete each word with the correct vowel team.

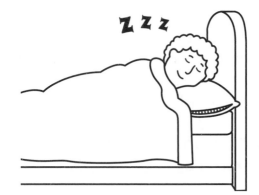

1. What do you do when you are tired?

   sl ____ ____ p

2. This is water that falls from the sky.

   r ____ ____ n

3. You use this in a bath.

   s ____ ____ p

4. Jack carried this up a hill.

   p ____ ____ l

5. You ride in this on water.

   b ____ ____ t

6. You play in the sand here.

   b ____ ____ ch

7. You do this with your eyes.

   s ____ ____

Draw a pennant shape on a card and write these vowel teams inside: *ai*, *ea*, *ee*, *oa*. Keep the card handy when you read with your child. Can your child find any words with the vowel teams? If so, say the words, stretching out the long vowel sound.

Helping at Home

# Compound Words

A **compound word** is a word made up of two or more words together. The joined words make a new word with a new meaning.

**Example:** butter + fly = butterfly

Use words in the word bank to form two-syllable compound words.

| air | ball | fire | house |
|-----|------|------|-------|
| road | sea | stick | suds |

1. rail _____

2. drum _____

3. soap _____

4. _____ plane

5. _____ shell

6. foot _____

7. _____ works

8. play _____

**Helping at Home**

Use compound words to make up addition and subtraction problems with your child. For example, say, "*Sea* plus *shell* equals *seashell*," or, "*Baseball* minus *base* equals *ball*."

# Verbs

**Verbs** are action words. Verbs can have an ending that shows they are an action happening now. The ending is *-ing*.

**Example:** Sometimes, I find my toys. Right now, I am find**ing** my toys.

Look at the verbs below. Write the verb with *-ing* on the end of the word to show it is being done right now.

| Sometimes, I... | Right now, I am... |
|---|---|
| 1. talk | |
| 2. sleep | |
| 3. watch | |
| 4. cook | |
| 5. cry | |
| 6. clean | |
| 7. jump | |
| 8. mix | |

What if you do something tomorrow? You use an extra verb, *will*. Use a verb from above and complete the sentences.

9. I will _____ .

10. I will _____ .

**Helping at Home**

Name an object such as an apple. Take turns with your child telling serious or silly things you are doing with it. For example, say, "I am biting the apple," or "I am dancing with the apple." Make sure each action word ends in *–ing*.

# Verbs

**Verbs** are action words. Verbs can have an ending that shows they were an action done in the past. The ending is -ed.

**Example:** Today, I yell for Mom. Yesterday, I yell<u>ed</u> for Mom.

Look at the verbs below. Write the verb with -ed on the end of the word to show it was done yesterday.

| Today, I… | Yesterday, I… |
|---|---|
| 1. pull | |
| 2. pick | |
| 3. ask | |
| 4. want | |
| 5. look | |
| 6. help | |
| 7. turn | |
| 8. climb | |

What if you do something tomorrow? Use an extra verb, _will_. Pick two verbs and complete the sentences.

9. I will _____ .

10. I will _____ .

**Make up funny stories with your child about the adventures of Yolanda Yesterday, Tony Today, and Tracey Tomorrow. For each story, keep all verbs in the present (example: _help_), past (example: _helped_), or future tense (example: _will help_).**

# Irregular Words

Some words are not spelled the way they sound. These words are called **irregular** words. They have their own spelling.

**Example:** The word *was* sounds like it should be spelled *wuz*.

Read the irregular words aloud. Write a sentence next to each one.

| Irregular Word | Sentence |
|---|---|
| 1. they | |
| 2. your | |
| 3. because | |
| 4. enough | |
| 5. were | |
| 6. one | |
| 7. know | |

Helping at Home

Write a short message to your child that includes a phonetic spelling in place of a correct spelling. For example, write *You wir so good today!* Let your child fix your mistake and write a return message to you.

# Writing an Opinion

Sometimes, you want readers to agree with what you think. You want them to agree with your **opinion**. Your opinion shows how you feel about a topic.

Think about this question: Should students get 30 minutes of free time at school each day?

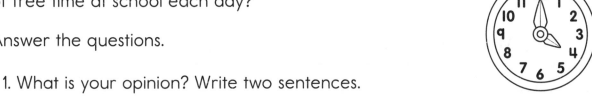

Answer the questions.

1. What is your opinion? Write two sentences.

   _____

   _____

2. Who are you trying to persuade? Why? Write two sentences.

   _____

   _____

3. Why should others agree with you? List two reasons that support your opinion.

   A. _____

   B. _____

4. Write an ending sentence for your opinion.

   Finally, others should agree with me because _____

   _____

   _____ .

When your child asks for something, ask him or her to give several reasons why you should agree. Ask questions that will help your child fully express an opinion. Finally, help your child compose an e-mail to make the request officially.

# Writing to Inform

You can use facts, reasons, and examples to explain topics in your writing. A topic is what you write about.

Read the prompt. Use the charts to help you write about your favorite subject.

**Topic**

My favorite subject is _____.

Why is it your favorite? Give a reason.

_____

_____

_____

Why is it your favorite? Give another reason.

_____

_____

_____

Tell me more! Give an example.

_____

_____

_____

Tell me more! Give an example.

_____

_____

_____

**Ending**

_____

_____

_____

Encourage your child to write and illustrate a little book that tells all about a favorite animal, sport, or other topic. Prompt your child to include facts and details. Read the book together and tell your child how informative it is!

# Writing a Story

Think about a special event in your life. Fill in the chart with answers to the Five Ws.

| |
|---|
| What happened? |
| Who was there? |
| When did it happen? |
| Where did it happen? |
| Why did it happen? |

**Helping at Home**

Encourage your child to use the completed chart above to write a true story about a special event. It should include a beginning, a middle, and an ending. Your child may wish to dictate the story to you and then add illustrations.

# Journal Writing

**Journal writing** is a way to share ideas, thoughts, and feelings. It helps to start your sentences with time-order words, such as *first*, *then*, *after*, and *finally*. It gives your writing order.

Respond to the journal prompt.

What would you do if you were principal for the day?

| |
|---|
| First, _____. |
| Then, _____. |
| After, _____. |
| Finally, _____. |

Draw a picture of yourself as principal!

| |
|---|
| |

**Helping at Home**

Encourage your child to remove this page from the book and share it with his or her principal. It could be included in a card your child makes for the principal. Sharing writing with others, or publishing, is an important part of the writing process.

# Revising

You are going to write a story. In this story, a child will go ice-skating for the first time! The middle of the story has been written for you.

1. Write a beginning and an ending to finish the story.

| **Beginning** |
| --- |
| **Middle**<br>    We put our ice skates on. We walked to the skating rink. I grabbed Mom's hand and looked at the other children. They were laughing and having a great time! I took a deep breath. I stepped onto the ice for the first time. My mom helped me balance. I placed one foot in front of the other. |
| **End** |

2. Have a friend look at your beginning and your ending. Ask your friend to make suggestions about your writing. This can make your writing stronger. Your friend can use the checklist below.

| | |
| --- | --- |
| 1. How can the writer make the beginning better? | |
| 2. How can the writer make the ending better? | |
| 3. What do you like about what your friend wrote? | |

Review the suggestions for your child's writing. Help your child write the complete story again, incorporating responses to the suggestions. Talk about how the story changed and how it improved.

# Using Digital Tools

Everyone has different likes and experiences. Write three lists based on your life.

**Things I Can Do**

1. _____

2. _____

3. _____

**Games I Like to Play**

1. _____

2. _____

3. _____

**Places I Have Been**

1. _____

2. _____

3. _____

Type one list on the computer. Print a copy.

**Helping at Home**

Help your child name the file with the three lists and save it to his or her own folder on your computer. Encourage your child to re-open the file, add text, and save. Your child may wish to experiment with changing the font or adding clip art, too.

# Research

1. Find a friend.
2. Research the topic of winter. Look in books. Read winter Web sites.
3. Share information with your friend.
4. Complete the chart with details about winter.

**Topic:** Winter

| **Fact #1** | **Example for Fact #1** |
|---|---|
| _____ | _____ |
| _____ | _____ |
| _____ | _____ |

| **Fact #2** | **Example for Fact #2** |
|---|---|
| _____ | _____ |
| _____ | _____ |
| _____ | _____ |

| **Fact #3** | **Example for Fact #3** |
|---|---|
| _____ | _____ |
| _____ | _____ |
| _____ | _____ |

Helping at Home

Show your child how to fold and cut a sheet of white paper to make a snowflake. Encourage him or her to write the facts and examples about winter on the snowflake and display it.

# Journal Writing

Respond to each journal prompt.

What is the nicest thing that someone has done for you?

_____

_____

_____

_____

What is the nicest thing that you have done for someone else?

_____

_____

_____

_____

Encourage your child to respond to the journal prompts by writing freely, without pausing to think about handwriting or spelling. This will help your child focus on his or her ideas and develop fluency as a writer. Revising and editing can come later.

# Nouns

A **common noun** names a person, place, thing, or idea.

**Examples:** My <u>brother</u> set the <u>table</u> in the <u>dining room</u> with <u>love</u>.
(person)　　　　(thing)　　　　(place)　　　　(idea)

Write each common noun in the correct box below.

| bedroom | chair | dad | freedom |
| love | mother | school | swing |

| Person | Place | Thing | Idea |
|--------|-------|-------|------|
|        |       |       |      |

A **proper noun** names a special person, place, or thing. It begins with a capital letter.

**Examples:** <u>Timothy</u> lives in <u>Washington</u> with his dog <u>Ruffy</u>.
(person)　　　　(place)　　　　(thing)

Write each proper noun in the correct box below.

| America | Casey | Florida |
| Friday | January | Mrs. Wu |

| Person | Place | Thing |
|--------|-------|-------|
|        |       |       |

Think of a proper noun that is meaningful to your child, such as the name of the street you live on or the name of his or her birthday month. Go on a hunt to find the name five times anywhere in your home. Notice that it begins with a capital letter.

# Letters and Words

Write the alphabet below.

### Uppercase Letters

|  |  |  |  |  |  |  |
|--|--|--|--|--|--|--|
|  |  |  |  |  |  |  |
|  |  |  |  |  |  |  |
|  |  |  |  |  |  |  |

### Lowercase Letters

|  |  |  |  |  |  |  |
|--|--|--|--|--|--|--|
|  |  |  |  |  |  |  |
|  |  |  |  |  |  |  |
|  |  |  |  |  |  |  |

Fill in the chart. Circle the correct verbs to finish the sentences.

| Noun or Plural Noun | Verb Choices | End of the Sentence |
|---|---|---|
| 1. The buildings | *is*  or  *are* | very tall. |
| 2. Mother | *want*  or  *wants* | to go inside. |
| 3. The teacher | *write*  or  *writes* | on the board. |
| 4. Spike and Buddy | *eat*  or  *eats* | all of their dog food. |
| 5. East School | *is*  or  *are* | in my state. |

Check your answers. Read each sentence aloud. Make sure the sentences sound right.

# Adjectives

An **adjective** is a word that describes a person, place, thing, or idea.

**Examples:** a <u>large</u> man, a <u>small</u> room, a <u>sunny</u> day

Look at each pair of adjectives. Circle the adjective that describes the picture.

1. furry    rough

2. loud    late

3. rainy    round

4. boring    bumpy

5. tough    tiny

6. silly    sandy

7. strong    soft

8. sweet    shiny

Helping at Home

Give three adjectives to your child, such as *furry, brown,* and *energetic.* Can your child guess that you are describing the dog? Take turns giving describing words and guessing what is being described.

# Conjunctions

A **conjunction** is a word that joins together two sentences to make one long sentence. Some conjunctions are *and, or,* and *but.*

**Example:** I like the red car, <u>and</u> I like the blue car.

Join the two sentences. Use the conjunctions in the box. You can use each more than once.

| and | but | or |
|-----|-----|-----|

1. We're going to the fair, _____ we're going to the beach.

2. The beach is fun, _____ I like the rides at the fair.

3. I like to drive the small cars, _____ I like to wave at my mother.

4. She likes the games, _____ I love driving.

5. I'll pick the sports car, _____ I'll pick the truck.

6. The car is pretty, _____ the truck looks huge.

7. Maybe I can drive one, _____ then I can drive the other one.

8. I'll pick the red car, _____ I'll drive the blue truck later.

Helping at Home

Show your child how to draw a train car with connectors on each side around each conjunction he or she wrote on this page. This will visually reinforce the concept that conjunctions join two sentences together.

# Articles

A and *an* are special adjectives called **articles**. Use *a* to describe a singular noun that begins with a consonant sound. Use *an* to describe a singular noun that begins with a vowel or a vowel sound.

**Examples:** <u>a</u> coach, <u>an</u> ant

Write *a* or *an* in front of each noun.

1. _____ apple

2. _____ coconut

3. _____ banana

4. _____ zucchini

5. _____ orange

6. _____ pear

7. _____ eggplant

8. _____ pear

9. _____ pepper

10. _____ cherry

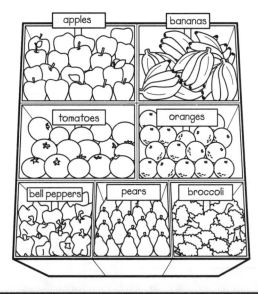

Say "a" and ask your child to say the name of an animal that begins with a consonant sound. Say "an" and ask your child to say the name of an animal that begins with a vowel sound. Keep playing until you have exhausted the possibilities.

# Prepositions

We use special words to show where something is. These words are called **prepositions**. They show where something is or what it is close to.

Use the prepositions in the box to complete the sentences.

| at | in | on |
|---|---|---|

1. I live _____ London.

2. The cat is _____ the table.

3. Sydney left the toy _____ her friend's house.

| across | around | behind |
|---|---|---|

4. The puzzle piece was _____ the couch.

5. The necklace is _____ her neck.

6. I yelled _____ the lake to my friend.

| down | inside | over |
|---|---|---|

7. We drove _____ the bridge.

8. It was time for dinner, so Gus went _____ to eat.

9. She rode her bike _____ the hill.

Helping at Home

Play a game with two toys such as an action figure and a car. Move the action figure around the car and ask your child to describe where it is. For example, the figure might be *above* the car, *beside* the car, *in* the car, or *behind* the car.

# Types of Sentences

Sentences come in four different types.

A **telling** sentence tells information. It ends with a period (.).

An **asking** sentence asks a question. It ends with a question mark (**?**).

An **exciting** sentence shows strong feelings. It ends with an exclamation point (**!**).

A **commanding** sentence gives an order. It ends with a period (.).

Identify the sentences. Write *T* for telling, *A* for asking, *E* for exciting, or *C* for commanding.

_____ 1. Do you have a new pet?

_____ 2. Yes, it was a birthday present!

_____ 3. What type of pet is it?

_____ 4. It is a beautiful calico kitten.

_____ 5. Wow, I have a calico kitten too!

_____ 6. Tell me about the cat.

_____ 7. She has a white belly.

_____ 8. Is she totally white?

_____ 9. No, she is black and brown.

_____ 10. Let me play with her.

Helping at Home

At the count of three, make a fist (period), raise your index finger (exclamation point), or curve your hand downward (question mark). Can your child think of a sentence that goes with that punctuation mark? Take turns.

# Pronouns

**Pronouns** take the place of nouns.

**Example:** <u>Mark</u> likes bikes. <u>He</u> likes bikes.

Use the word bank below. Replace the nouns with pronouns.

| He | It | She | They | We |

1. <u>Todd and I</u> will go to the mall. _____

2. <u>Grandma</u> will meet us there. _____

3. <u>Todd</u> wants to buy a shirt. _____

4. <u>The shirt</u> has to be blue. _____

5. <u>Grandma and Todd</u> will make sure it is the right size. _____

These sentences are in trouble! They are missing a capital letter at the beginning. They have a word spelled wrong. And, no punctuation is at the end. Fix the sentences below. Write the fixed sentences.

6. elias was going to the stor

_____

7. henry felt very hapy

_____

8. would you take me to the lak

_____

**Helping at Home**
Call out a person's name, several people's names, or an object. Challenge your child to respond with a pronoun that could take the name's place. Take turns giving names and pronouns. See how fast and long you can go without making an error.

# Commas

> Use a **comma** (,) to separate a series of three or more things in a sentence.
>
> **Example:** Juan has juice, yogurt, and carrots for his snack today.

Read the sentences. Add commas to separate three or more things in a series.

1. Rana bought eggs flour and butter to bake a cake.

2. Dad bought salad pears and bread at the grocery store.

3. I sit next to Joannie Grace and Sam in class.

4. My mom drives a yellow black and gray car.

5. The sandwich had turkey tomato and lettuce on wheat bread.

6. On vacation, Ned bought games puzzles and cards.

7. At the zoo, the children saw lions elephants and tigers.

8. We will need balloons cake and streamers for the party.

> Use a **comma** to separate the day from the year when writing the date.
>
> **Example:** March 24, 2013

9. February 4 2010                    10. November 12 2014

**Helping at Home**

Use short lengths of pipe cleaner to make comma shapes. Write a sentence from this page on a large sheet of paper. Invite your child to glue the commas in the appropriate spots. Talk about how commas hang a little bit below the line.

# Prefixes and Suffixes

A **prefix** is a word part that is at the beginning of some words. A prefix gives a clue to a word's meaning.

    **Example:** <u>Re</u>do means to do something again. The prefix *re-* means *again*.

Use the prefixes in the box. Fill in the blanks. Then, write what the word means.

| **pre-** | **re-** | **un-** |
|---|---|---|
| before | again | not |

1. _____view means to _____ .

2. _____tie means to _____ .

3. _____take means to _____ .

A **suffix** is a word part that is at the end of some words. A suffix gives a clue to a word's meaning.

    **Example:** Care<u>less</u> is to do something without care. The suffix *-less* means *without*.

Use the suffixes in the box. Fill in the blanks. Then, write what the word means.

| **-able** | **-ful** | **-less** |
|---|---|---|
| able to | full of | without |

4. Rest_____ means _____ .

5. Help_____ means _____ .

6. Build_____ means _____ .

Helping at Home

Write the prefixes and suffixes from this page on index cards and place them in a bag. Can your child draw a card and say a word that includes that word part? Take turns. You may wish to make a list of the new words you made.

# Categories

Words can be sorted into groups. These groups are called categories.
**Categories** show what things some words may have in common.

**Example:** Turkey, ham, and beef are all types of meat.

Sort the words in the word bank into the groups.

| apple | banana | bowl |
| coat | dish | fork |
| glove | hat | orange |
| pear | scarf | spoon |

| Fruits We Eat | Things We Wear in Cold Weather | Things We Use to Eat with |
|---|---|---|
| | | |
| | | |
| | | |
| | | |

Helping at Home

Play a silly game with your child. Take turns naming three things, such as *bread*, *butter*, and *pencil*. Ask, "Which one does not belong? Why not?"

# Categories

Words can be sorted into groups. These groups are called categories.
**Categories** show what things some words may have in common.

**Example:** Circles, squares, and triangles are all types of shapes.

Sort the words in the word bank into the groups.

| | | |
|---|---|---|
| bobcat | duck | goose |
| iguana | jaguar | lion |
| lizard | penguin | snake |
| swan | tiger | turtle |

| Birds That Swim | Large Cats | Green Reptiles |
|---|---|---|
| | | |
| | | |
| | | |
| | | |

Gather a group of toys, buttons, socks, or other small objects. Invite your child to categorize them in different ways: by size, shape, pattern, or type. Encourage your child to explain each sorting strategy.

# Categories

Words can be sorted into groups. These groups are called categories. **Categories** show what things some words may have in common.

**Example:** Dolls, teddy bears, and blocks are all types of toys.

Sort the words in the word bank into the groups.

| | | |
|---|---|---|
| bike | broccoli | car |
| chocolate | cucumber | lettuce |
| mint | peas | skateboard |
| strawberry | tricycle | vanilla |

| Green Vegetables | Things with Wheels | Ice-Cream Flavors |
|---|---|---|
| | | |
| | | |
| | | |
| | | |

Write these 12 words on index cards: *the, they, three, ago, asks, again, fun, five, flips, why, when, water.* Challenge your child to sort the words in two different ways.

# Shades of Meaning

Words have **shades of meaning**. They can mean almost the same thing but make the reader think different things. Think about how the underlined words are the same and different.

Drew <u>sipped</u> his water.
Drew <u>gulped</u> his water.

Find a partner. Act out each word below. Have fun!

| | | |
|---|---|---|
| 1. walk | march | prance |
| 2. whisper | talk | shout |
| 3. look | stare | glance |
| 4. pat | tap | poke |
| 5. jump | skip | hop |
| 6. cool | chilly | freezing |
| 7. warm | hot | boiling |
| 8. touch | grab | snatch |

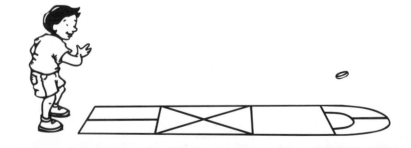

Helping
at Home

When you read a story with your child, pause when you come to verbs such as *said, ran, laughed,* or *shouted.* For each verb, challenge your child to supply another word with a similar or related meaning.

# Words from Reading

Read the story.

## Aunt Jill

Everyone can have a **special** person in his or her life. The special person can be a friend or family member. Pets can be special, too! Aunt Jill is my special person. She likes to draw pictures. She uses **different** colors. She plays the piano. Aunt Jill bakes cookies in the oven. She eats peanut butter cookies. Aunt Jill's **smile** makes her special. She is always laughing. She is very happy. She is my special person.

Write a sentence for each word from the story.

| Word | Sentence |
| --- | --- |
| special | |
| different | |
| smile | |

**Helping at Home**

Have your child choose three words from the story about Aunt Jill. Encourage your child to use those words to write several sentences about a person who is special to him or her. Mail the writing to the special person.

# Common Core State Standards for Math*

The following parent-friendly explanations of first grade Common Core math standards are provided to help you understand what your child will learn in school this year. Practice pages listed will help your child master each skill.

Complete Common Core State Standards may be found here: www.corestandards.org.

## 1.OA Operations and Algebraic Thinking

### Represent and solve problems involving addition and subtraction.
### (Standards: 1.OA.A.1, 1.OA.A.2)

*Your child will use addition and subtraction within 20 to solve word problems that involve adding to, taking from, putting together, taking apart, and comparing. Your child will represent problems using drawings and standard math problems.* • **Practice pages: 68–72, 76, 77, 87**

*Your child will solve word problems that require adding three numbers whose sum is less than 20.* • **Practice pages: 71, 72**

### Understand and apply properties of operations and the relationship
### between addition and subtraction. Add and subtract within 20.
### (Standards: 1.OA.B.3, 1.OA.B.4, 1.OA.C.5, 1.OA.C.6 )

*Your child will think about addition in a variety of ways. For example, numbers can be added by counting up, by making a ten (for 3 + 6 + 4, 6 and 4 can be added first to make 10), by rearranging (since 7 + 4 = 11, then 4 + 7 = 11), by thinking about related subtraction problems (since 10 − 3 = 7, then 7 + 3 = 10), and by thinking of related problems that are easier (6 + 7 is the same as 6 + 6 + 1).* • **Practice pages: 69, 73, 74, 77, 79–82, 86**

*Your child will think about subtraction in a variety of ways. For example, numbers can be subtracted by counting backward, by finding the number that makes a ten (solve 10 − 6 by finding the number that makes 10 when added to 6), by thinking about related addition problems (since 9 + 2 = 11, then 11 − 2 = 9), and by breaking down a problem into easier problems (15 − 6 = 15 − 5 − 1 = 10 − 1 = 9).* • **Practice pages: 70, 73–76, 78, 82–84, 86, 88**

**Work with addition and subtraction equations.**
**(Standards: 1.OA.D.7, 1.OA.D.8)**

*Your child will understand the meaning of the equal sign (=) and use it to write and solve addition and subtraction problems. He or she will decide whether problems as written are true or false.* • **Practice pages: 68, 86, 88**

*Your child will determine the missing number in an addition or subtraction problem.* • **Practice pages: 84, 85, 87**

## 1.NBT Number and Operations in Base Ten

**Extend the counting sequence.**
**(Standard: 1.NBT.A.1)**

*Your child will count to 120 starting from any number and write numbers to 120.* • **Practice pages: 89–93**

**Understand place value.**
**(Standards: 1.NBT.B.2a, 1.NBT.B.2b, 1.NBT.B.2c, 1.NBT.B.3)**

*Your child will understand that a two-digit number is made up of tens and ones. A ten can be thought of as a bundle of 10 ones.* • **Practice pages: 94–97**

*Your child will work with numbers 11–19 and understand that they are made up of 1 ten plus 1–9 ones.* • **Practice pages: 94–97, 104, 105**

*Your child will understand that the numbers 10, 20, 30, 40, 50, 60, 70, 80 and 90 are made up of 1–9 tens and 0 ones.* • **Practice page: 98**

*Your child will compare two-digit numbers by thinking about how many tens and ones they contain. He or she will decide which number is greater or less.* • **Practice pages: 99, 100**

# Common Core State Standards for Math*

**Use place value understanding and properties of operations to add and subtract.**
**(Standards: 1.NBT.C.4, 1.NBT.C.5, 1.NBT.C.6)**

Your child will use an understanding of ones and tens to add two-digit numbers within 100. He or she will begin to add numbers in which regrouping (or "carrying a ten") is required.
• **Practice pages:** 101, 103–105

Your child will mentally find 10 more or 10 less than a given number (for example, 52 – 10 = 42) and explain the strategy used. • **Practice pages:** 101, 102, 103

Your child will subtract multiples of 10 (for example, 80 – 30). • **Practice pages:** 102, 103

## 1.MD Measurement and Data

**Measure lengths indirectly and by iterating length units.**
**(Standards: 1.MD.A.1, 1.MD.A.2)**

Your child will compare the lengths of objects and put them in order by length.
• **Practice pages:** 106, 108

Your child will use a non-standard unit of measurement (for example, a paper clip) to measure the length of objects. • **Practice pages:** 107, 108

**Tell and write time.**
**(Standard: 1.MD.B.3)**

Your child will tell and write time in hours and half-hours using both digital and analog clocks.
• **Practice pages:** 109–111

**Represent and interpret data.**
**(Standard: 1.MD.C.4)**

*Your child will organize information into categories. He or she will use the organized data to answer questions like these: Which category has most? Which has least? How many more are in one category than another?* • **Practice pages:** 112–114

# 1.G Geometry

**Reason with shapes and their attributes.**
**(Standards: 1.G.A.1, 1.G.A.2, 1.G.A.3)**

*Your child will look at shapes and their features. He or she will notice how many sides each shape has, how many corners it has, etc.* • **Practice pages:** 115–117

*Your child will put two-dimensional shapes (square, triangle, circle) or three-dimensional shapes (cubes, cylinders, spheres) together to form larger, composite shapes.*
• **Practice page:** 117

*Your child will notice when shapes are divided equally and unequally. He or she will divide circles and rectangles into two or four equal parts and describe the parts using the terms halves, fourths, and quarters. This standard helps your child begin to understand fractions.*
• **Practice pages:** 118–121

# Equations

The picture shows a group of 4 dogs and a group of 3 dogs. The picture also shows 7 dogs in all. Another way to write this is 4 + 3 = 7. This is called an **equation**. An equation is the same on both sides of the **equal sign** (=).

Write an equation for each group of objects.

1.

_____ + _____ = _____

2.

_____ + _____ = _____

3.

_____ + _____ = _____

4.

_____ + _____ = _____

5.

_____ + _____ = _____

6.

_____ + _____ = _____

**Helping at Home**

Help your child put one sticker on one index card, two stickers on another index card, etc., until he or she has cards for 1–10. On three more index cards, write +, -, and =. Challenge your child to use the cards to make equations.

# Addition

Two carrots and three carrots make five carrots in all. Another way to say this is 2 plus 3 equals 5. Five is the **sum**.
Color 2 carrots green.
Color 3 carrots orange.
How many carrots are there in all?

$$\begin{array}{r} 2 \\ +\ 3 \\ \hline \boxed{5} \end{array}$$

Color the pictures. Count the objects. Solve each problem.

1. Color 1 party hat blue.
   Color 3 party hats red.
   How many party hats
   are there in all?

   $$\begin{array}{r} 1 \\ +\ 3 \\ \hline \square \end{array}$$

2. Color 4 apples red.
   Color 2 apples yellow.
   How many apples are
   there in all?

   $$\begin{array}{r} 4 \\ +\ 2 \\ \hline \square \end{array}$$

3. Color 2 stars yellow.
   Color 2 stars blue.
   How many stars are
   there in all?

   $$\begin{array}{r} 2 \\ +\ 2 \\ \hline \square \end{array}$$

4. Color 1 balloon red.
   Color 4 balloons yellow.
   How many balloons are
   there in all?

   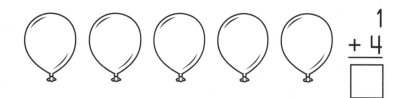

   $$\begin{array}{r} 1 \\ +\ 4 \\ \hline \square \end{array}$$

**Helping at Home**

Give more addition and subtraction equations related to the pictures. For example, for the party hats, give *3 + 1 = 4* or *4 – 1 = 3*. Can your child point to the set of objects that illustrate the equation you gave? Have your child give you equations, too.

# Subtraction

There were 8 books. Take away 2 books.
How many books were left?
Eight books take away 2 books
leaves 6 books. Six is the **difference**.

$$8 - 2 = 6$$

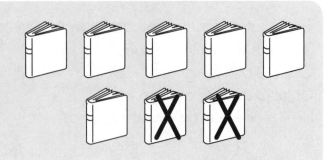

Cross out and count the objects. Solve each problem.

1. There are 2 sailboats.
   Take away 1 sailboat.
   How many sailboats are left?

   $2 - 1 =$ _____

2. There are 5 birds.
   Take away 3 birds.
   How many birds are left?

   $5 - 3 =$ _____

3. There are 3 cookies.
   Take away 2 cookies.
   How many cookies are left?

   $3 - 2 =$ _____

4. There are 6 bananas.
   Take away 2 bananas.
   How many bananas are left?

   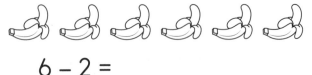

   $6 - 2 =$ _____

5. There are 7 rabbits.
   Take away 4 rabbits.
   How many rabbits are left?

   $7 - 4 =$ _____

6. There are 8 flowers.
   Take away 3 flowers.
   How many flowers are left?

   $8 - 3 =$ _____

**Helping at Home**

Encourage your child to make up a story to accompany each
subtraction problem on the page. To help, ask questions such as,
"Who ate the two bananas?" and "Where did the four rabbits go when
they hopped away?"

# Word Problems

Some words in a **word problem** tell you whether to add or subtract. These key words tell you to add: *altogether*, *total*, *in all*, and *combined*. After you solve a problem, label the answer with the correct unit.

**Example:** Kim has 4 green rubber bands and 7 red rubber bands. How many rubber bands does she have in all?

4 + 7 = 11 rubber bands

Circle the key words in each word problem. Write an equation to find the answer. Label the answer with the correct units.

| | |
|---|---|
| 1. Anna counted 6 red crayons and 2 blue crayons. How many total crayons did Anna count? _____ | 2. Lauren has 8 pencils and Keisha has 7 pencils. How many pencils do they have combined? _____ |
| 3. Clay found 5 small paper clips and 3 large paper clips. How many paper clips did he find altogether? _____ | 4. Delia counted 5 black pens, 2 red pens, and 1 blue pen. How many pens did she count in all? _____ |
| 5. Dante has 7 pink erasers and 2 green erasers. How many total erasers does Dante have? _____ | 6. Blake borrowed 3 blue markers, 4 yellow markers, and 3 green markers. How many markers did he borrow in all? _____ |

**Helping at Home**

Have your child choose two word problems from the page to act out either by finding and manipulating objects found around the house or by drawing the objects described in the problem.

# Word Problems

Solve each problem. Write the equation across or in a column.

1. Lily ate 3 carrots on Friday, 4 carrots on Saturday, and 5 carrots on Sunday. How many carrots did she eat in all?

$$+$$

2. Jayla has 6 pencils. Her brother has 7 pencils. How many pencils do they have altogether?

_____ + _____ = _____

3. Robert has 5 fish. His friend Alex has 9 fish. How many total fish do they have?

_____ + _____ = _____

4. Lori used 2 cans of paint on the doghouse, 8 cans of paint on the fence, and 3 cans of paint on the playhouse. How many cans of paint did Lori use altogether?

$$+$$

5. Abbie walked 5 miles on Monday, 4 miles on Tuesday, and 8 miles on Wednesday. How many miles did she walk in all?

$$+$$

6. Eight butterflies are on a bush. Seven more butterflies land on the bush. How many total butterflies are on the bush?

_____ + _____ = _____

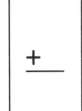

Write several word problems about topics that are meaningful to your child. They could be about friends, toys, a favorite activity, or something that happens to a favorite fictional character. Solve the problems together.

# Number Families

Write the equations for each number family.

**1.**

$$\underline{\quad 3 \quad} + \underline{\quad 1 \quad} = \underline{\quad 4 \quad}$$

$$\underline{\qquad} + \underline{\qquad} = \underline{\qquad}$$

$$\underline{\qquad} - \underline{\qquad} = \underline{\qquad}$$

$$\underline{\qquad} - \underline{\qquad} = \underline{\qquad}$$

**2.**

⬤ 5 3 2

$$\underline{\qquad} + \underline{\qquad} = \underline{\qquad}$$

$$\underline{\qquad} + \underline{\qquad} = \underline{\qquad}$$

$$\underline{\qquad} - \underline{\qquad} = \underline{\qquad}$$

$$\underline{\qquad} - \underline{\qquad} = \underline{\qquad}$$

**3.**

⬤ 1 3 2

$$\underline{\qquad} + \underline{\qquad} = \underline{\qquad}$$

$$\underline{\qquad} + \underline{\qquad} = \underline{\qquad}$$

$$\underline{\qquad} - \underline{\qquad} = \underline{\qquad}$$

$$\underline{\qquad} - \underline{\qquad} = \underline{\qquad}$$

**4.**

⬤ 4 2 6

$$\underline{\qquad} + \underline{\qquad} = \underline{\qquad}$$

$$\underline{\qquad} + \underline{\qquad} = \underline{\qquad}$$

$$\underline{\qquad} - \underline{\qquad} = \underline{\qquad}$$

$$\underline{\qquad} - \underline{\qquad} = \underline{\qquad}$$

**Helping at Home**

Challenge your child to think of numbers that make up two more number families. Have your child use each number family to create four addition and subtraction problems for you to solve. Have your child check your work.

# Number Families

Write the equations for each number family.

1.

$$\left(\begin{array}{c} 7 \\ 10 \quad 3 \end{array}\right)$$

_____ + _____ = _____

_____ + _____ = _____

_____ − _____ = _____

_____ − _____ = _____

2.

$$\left(\begin{array}{c} 8 \\ 12 \quad 4 \end{array}\right)$$

_____ + _____ = _____

_____ + _____ = _____

_____ − _____ = _____

_____ − _____ = _____

3.

$$\left(\begin{array}{c} 9 \\ 13 \quad 4 \end{array}\right)$$

_____ + _____ = _____

_____ + _____ = _____

_____ − _____ = _____

_____ − _____ = _____

4.

$$\left(\begin{array}{c} 6 \\ 11 \quad 5 \end{array}\right)$$

_____ + _____ = _____

_____ + _____ = _____

_____ − _____ = _____

_____ − _____ = _____

5.

$$\left(\begin{array}{c} 5 \\ 13 \quad 8 \end{array}\right)$$

_____ + _____ = _____

_____ + _____ = _____

_____ − _____ = _____

_____ − _____ = _____

6.

$$\left(\begin{array}{c} 4 \\ 11 \quad 7 \end{array}\right)$$

_____ + _____ = _____

_____ + _____ = _____

_____ − _____ = _____

_____ − _____ = _____

**Helping at Home**
On a sheet of paper, draw a family of four ants. Each ant should have three large body sections. Then, invite your child to use the three numbers in a number family to write an addition or subtraction equation on each ant.

# Subtraction Strategies

Subtract. Count the shapes on the flags for help.

1.
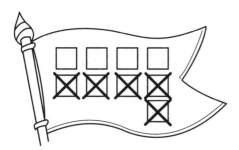

9 – 5 = _____

2.

8 – 4 = _____

3.
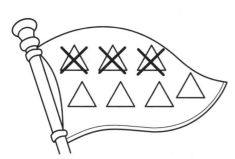

7 – 3 = _____

4.
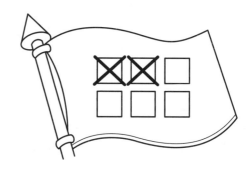

6 – 2 = _____

5.

9 – 3 = _____

6.
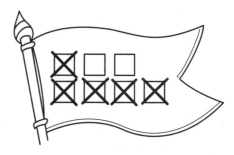

7 – 5 = _____

**Helping at Home**

Have your child begin to count 10 pennies. At a random time, say, "Stop!" Then, your child must write a subtraction equation based on the current count. For example, he or she might write *10 – 2 = 8*. Play again, this time having your child tell you to stop.

# Subtraction Strategies

Sometimes, it helps to cross off the number of objects to be subtracted. Then, count the objects left.

**Example:** Josh had 12 marbles. He lost 5 marbles. How many marbles does Josh have left?

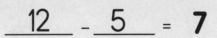

$$\underline{\quad 12 \quad} - \underline{\quad 5 \quad} = \mathbf{7}$$

Count back to solve each problem. Write the equation.

1. Nick had 7 coins. 4 rolled away. How many coins are left?

_____ – _____ = _____

2. Nora had 9 candies. She ate 2. How many candies are left?

_____ – _____ = _____

3. Mohammed has 11 books. He read 5 of them. How many books does he have left to read?

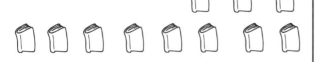

_____ – _____ = _____

4. We were feeding 8 fish in the pond. Three swam away. How many fish were left?

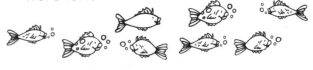

_____ – _____ = _____

5. Uncle Mario sent Dion 10 shells. When they arrived, 5 were broken. How many shells were not broken?

_____ – _____ = _____

6. There were 12 eggs in the refrigerator. Mom used 3 eggs for the cake. How many eggs were left?

_____ – _____ = _____

**Helping at Home**

Put 12 small toys in the cups of an empty egg carton. Take away several toys and ask your child to tell you the related subtraction equation, such as *12 – 3 = 9*. Act out addition problems, too. Your child may wish to make up stories about the equations.

# Addition Strategies

Start with the larger number and count on to add. Write the sum. Count the total shapes to check your answer.

1. 

$$\underline{\quad 15 \quad} + \underline{\quad\quad} = \underline{\quad\quad}$$

2. 

$$\underline{\quad 9 \quad} + \underline{\quad\quad} = \underline{\quad\quad}$$

3. 

$$\underline{\quad 11 \quad} + \underline{\quad\quad} = \underline{\quad\quad}$$

4. 

$$\underline{\quad 8 \quad} + \underline{\quad\quad} = \underline{\quad\quad}$$

5. 

$$\underline{\quad 14 \quad} + \underline{\quad\quad} = \underline{\quad\quad}$$

6. 

$$\underline{\quad 8 \quad} + \underline{\quad\quad} = \underline{\quad\quad}$$

7. 

$$\underline{\quad 9 \quad} + \underline{\quad\quad} = \underline{\quad\quad}$$

8. 

$$\underline{\quad 12 \quad} + \underline{\quad\quad} = \underline{\quad\quad}$$

9. 

$$\underline{\quad 10 \quad} + \underline{\quad\quad} = \underline{\quad\quad}$$

10. 

$$\underline{\quad 11 \quad} + \underline{\quad\quad} = \underline{\quad\quad}$$

**Helping at Home**

Go on a counting tour of your home. Count one set of items, such as forks or pillows. Then, find another set of items to add to your count. How high can you count? You may wish to use a notebook during your tour to write a long addition equation.

# Subtraction Strategies

Counting back along a number line helps to subtract larger numbers.

**Example:** 17 – 9 = 8

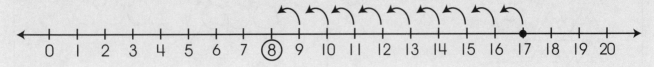

Subtract. Use the number line to count back.

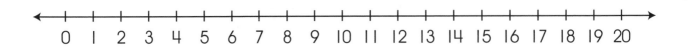

1. 15
   – 8

2. 16
   – 7

3. 12
   – 5

4. 17
   – 9

5. 17
   – 8

6. 13
   – 6

7. 15
   – 6

8. 16
   – 8

9. 12
   – 7

10. 16
    – 9

11. 14
    – 8

12. 15
    – 7

Use masking tape to create a giant number line on the floor inside, or sidewalk chalk to create one outside. Give subtraction problems and invite your child to walk or jump along the line to find the answer.

Helping at Home

# Addition Strategies

Adding doubles is often easier than adding 2 different numbers. Change the numbers to make them doubles or 1 more than a double. Add the double and, if there is a leftover, add 1 more.

**Example:** $3 + 5 = 4 + 4 = 8$    $2 + 5 = 3 + 3 + 1 = 7$

Move the dots to make doubles or near doubles. Add.

1.

$4 + 2 = $ _____

2.

$5 + 7 = $ _____

3.

$4 + 6 = $ _____

4.

$6 + 3 = $ _____ $+ $ _____ $+ 1 = $ _____

5.

$8 + 5 = $ _____ $+ $ _____ $+ 1 = $ _____

6.

$8 + 6 = $ _____ $+ $ _____ $= $ _____

7.

$9 + 6 = $ _____ $+ $ _____ $+ 1 = $ _____

**Helping at Home**

Roll a pair of dice with your child. Can the dots in each roll be rearranged to form doubles or near-doubles? If so, write a matching addition equation.

# Addition Strategies

$7 + 6 = 10 + 3 = 13$

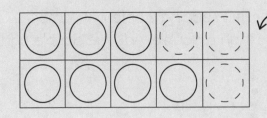 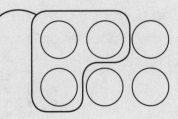

Use the tens frames to rewrite each problem with a ten. Add.

1. $8 + 7 = 10 +$ _____ = _____

2. $6 + 5 = 10 +$ _____ = _____

3. $7 + 4 = 10 +$ _____ = _____

4. $9 + 8 = 10 +$ _____ = _____

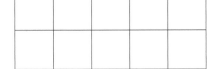

5. $8 + 6 = 10 +$ _____ = _____

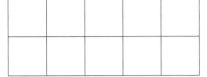

6. $7 + 5 = 10 +$ _____ = _____

**Helping at Home**

Raise a number of fingers greater than five and have your child do the same. Invite your child to lower some of your fingers and transfer the count to his or her fingers to total 10. How many of your fingers remain raised in addition to 10?

# Addition Strategies

When adding three numbers, look for a problem you already know and add those numbers. Then, add the third number to their sum.

**Example:**

$$
\begin{array}{r}
7 \\
3 \\
+5 \\
\end{array} \Big\rangle\ 10
\qquad
\begin{array}{r}
+5 \\
\hline
15
\end{array}
$$

7 and 3 make 10
add 5 to 10
10 + 5 = 15

Add.

1.
$$
\begin{array}{r}
6 \\
4 \\
+2 \\
\hline
\end{array}
$$

2.
$$
\begin{array}{r}
5 \\
2 \\
+5 \\
\hline
\end{array}
$$

3.
$$
\begin{array}{r}
5 \\
4 \\
+6 \\
\hline
\end{array}
$$

4.
$$
\begin{array}{r}
7 \\
2 \\
+3 \\
\hline
\end{array}
$$

5.
$$
\begin{array}{r}
4 \\
3 \\
+7 \\
\hline
\end{array}
$$

6.
$$
\begin{array}{r}
8 \\
6 \\
+2 \\
\hline
\end{array}
$$

7.
$$
\begin{array}{r}
2 \\
8 \\
+7 \\
\hline
\end{array}
$$

8.
$$
\begin{array}{r}
1 \\
8 \\
+9 \\
\hline
\end{array}
$$

**Helping at Home**

Play with magnetic numbers. Think aloud with your child as you add three numbers. For example, when adding the numbers 4, 4, and 2, say, "I know that four plus four equals eight, and that two more than eight is 10, so the answer must be 10."

# Addition and Subtraction

Add or subtract to complete each table. The first one has been started for you.

1.
Rule: +6

| In | Out |
|----|-----|
| 0 | **6** |
| 4 | **10** |
| 6 | **12** |
| 3 | |
| 1 | |
| 5 | |

2.
Rule: –2

| In | Out |
|----|-----|
| 4 | |
| 2 | |
| 10 | |
| 5 | |
| 7 | |
| 3 | |

3.
Rule: +4

| In | Out |
|----|-----|
| 2 | |
| 4 | |
| 1 | |
| 3 | |
| 8 | |
| 9 | |

4.
Rule: –3

| In | Out |
|----|-----|
| 3 | |
| 5 | |
| 6 | |
| 12 | |
| 7 | |
| 4 | |

5.
Rule: +8

| In | Out |
|----|-----|
| 4 | |
| 2 | |
| 1 | |
| 0 | |
| 5 | |
| 7 | |

6.
Rule: –1

| In | Out |
|----|-----|
| 4 | |
| 7 | |
| 8 | |
| 1 | |
| 10 | |
| 5 | |

**Helping at Home**

As your child completes the page, make several filled-in tables of your own, but do not include the rule you used to make them. Can your child examine the tables you made and determine the rule? Ask your child to make a table for you, too.

## Subtraction Strategies

It is easier to subtract 10 from a two-digit number. Figure out how much to add to the smaller number to make 10. Add the same to the larger number. Subtract.

**Example:** 13 − 8 → Think 8 + 2 = 10, so add 2 to both numbers and subtract.

$$13 + 2 = 15$$
$$\underline{-\ 8 + 2 = 10}$$
$$5$$

so 13 − 8 = 5

Add to make a ten and subtract.

1.     18 +          =
     − 9 +          = _____

2.     14 +          =
     − 6 +          = _____

3.     11 +          =
     − 4 +          = _____

4.     15 +          =
     − 7 +          = _____

5.     17 +          =
     − 8 +          = _____

6.     12 +          =
     − 5 +          = _____

**Helping at Home**

Think aloud while solving a problem on the page together. For the first problem, say, "Nine is the smaller number, and nine plus one equals 10. I need to add one to 18, too. Nineteen minus 10 equals nine, so 18 minus nine must equal nine, too."

# Subtraction Strategies

Solve each problem. Look for patterns.

1.

**13**

$13 - \underline{0} = 13$

$13 - \underline{\phantom{0}} = 12$

$13 - \underline{\phantom{0}} = 11$

$13 - \underline{\phantom{0}} = 10$

$13 - \underline{\phantom{0}} = 9$

$13 - 5 = \underline{\phantom{0}}$

$13 - 6 = \underline{\phantom{0}}$

$13 - 7 = \underline{\phantom{0}}$

$13 - \underline{\phantom{0}} = 5$

$13 - \underline{\phantom{0}} = 4$

$13 - \underline{\phantom{0}} = 3$

$13 - 11 = \underline{\phantom{0}}$

$13 - 12 = \underline{\phantom{0}}$

$13 - \underline{\phantom{0}} = 0$

2.

**14**

$14 - \underline{\phantom{0}} = 14$

$14 - 1 = \underline{\phantom{0}}$

$14 - \underline{\phantom{0}} = 12$

$14 - \underline{\phantom{0}} = 11$

$14 - 4 = \underline{\phantom{0}}$

$14 - 5 = \underline{\phantom{0}}$

$14 - 6 = \underline{\phantom{0}}$

$14 - \underline{\phantom{0}} = 7$

$14 - \underline{\phantom{0}} = 6$

$14 - \underline{\phantom{0}} = 5$

$14 - \underline{\phantom{0}} = 4$

$14 - 11 = \underline{\phantom{0}}$

$14 - 12 = \underline{\phantom{0}}$

$14 - \underline{\phantom{0}} = 1$

$14 - \underline{\phantom{0}} = 0$

3.

**15**

$15 - 0 = \underline{\phantom{0}}$

$15 - \underline{\phantom{0}} = 14$

$15 - 2 = \underline{\phantom{0}}$

$15 - \underline{\phantom{0}} = 12$

$15 - 4 = \underline{\phantom{0}}$

$15 - \underline{\phantom{0}} = 10$

$15 - \underline{\phantom{0}} = 9$

$15 - 7 = \underline{\phantom{0}}$

$15 - 8 = \underline{\phantom{0}}$

$15 - 9 = \underline{\phantom{0}}$

$15 - \underline{\phantom{0}} = 5$

$15 - \underline{\phantom{0}} = 4$

$15 - \underline{\phantom{0}} = 3$

$15 - 13 = \underline{\phantom{0}}$

$15 - 14 = \underline{\phantom{0}}$

$15 - \underline{\phantom{0}} = 0$

**Helping at Home**

Demonstrate the third set of problems on the page using 15 pennies. For each problem, subtract one more penny and write the answer in the blank. You may wish to continue by adding one penny at a time to make 15.

# Addition Strategies

Solve each problem. Look for patterns.

1.

### 16

$16 + \underline{\hspace{1cm}} = 16$

$15 + \underline{\hspace{1cm}} = 16$

$14 + \underline{\hspace{1cm}} = 16$

$\underline{\hspace{1cm}} + 3 = 16$

$\underline{\hspace{1cm}} + 4 = 16$

$11 + \underline{\hspace{1cm}} = 16$

$10 + \underline{\hspace{1cm}} = 16$

$9 + \underline{\hspace{1cm}} = 16$

$\underline{\hspace{1cm}} + 8 = 16$

$7 + \underline{\hspace{1cm}} = 16$

$\underline{\hspace{1cm}} + 10 = 16$

$5 + \underline{\hspace{1cm}} = 16$

$\underline{\hspace{1cm}} + 12 = 16$

$3 + \underline{\hspace{1cm}} = 16$

$\underline{\hspace{1cm}} + 14 = 16$

$1 + \underline{\hspace{1cm}} = 16$

$\underline{\hspace{1cm}} + 16 = 16$

2.

### 17

$17 + \underline{\hspace{1cm}} = 17$

$16 + \underline{\hspace{1cm}} = 17$

$\underline{\hspace{1cm}} + 2 = 17$

$14 + \underline{\hspace{1cm}} = 17$

$\underline{\hspace{1cm}} + 4 = 17$

$12 + \underline{\hspace{1cm}} = 17$

$11 + \underline{\hspace{1cm}} = 17$

$\underline{\hspace{1cm}} + 7 = 17$

$9 + \underline{\hspace{1cm}} = 17$

$\underline{\hspace{1cm}} + 9 = 17$

$7 + \underline{\hspace{1cm}} = 17$

$6 + \underline{\hspace{1cm}} = 17$

$5 + \underline{\hspace{1cm}} = 17$

$\underline{\hspace{1cm}} + 13 = 17$

$3 + \underline{\hspace{1cm}} = 17$

$2 + \underline{\hspace{1cm}} = 17$

$1 + \underline{\hspace{1cm}} = 17$

$0 + \underline{\hspace{1cm}} = 17$

3.

### 18

$18 + \underline{\hspace{1cm}} = 18$

$\underline{\hspace{1cm}} + 1 = 18$

$\underline{\hspace{1cm}} + 2 = 18$

$\underline{\hspace{1cm}} + 3 = 18$

$14 + \underline{\hspace{1cm}} = 18$

$13 + \underline{\hspace{1cm}} = 18$

$\underline{\hspace{1cm}} + 6 = 18$

$\underline{\hspace{1cm}} + 7 = 18$

$10 + \underline{\hspace{1cm}} = 18$

$9 + \underline{\hspace{1cm}} = 18$

$8 + \underline{\hspace{1cm}} = 18$

$7 + \underline{\hspace{1cm}} = 18$

$\underline{\hspace{1cm}} + 12 = 18$

$\underline{\hspace{1cm}} + 13 = 18$

$\underline{\hspace{1cm}} + 14 = 18$

$3 + \underline{\hspace{1cm}} = 18$

$2 + \underline{\hspace{1cm}} = 18$

$\underline{\hspace{1cm}} + 17 = 18$

$0 + \underline{\hspace{1cm}} = 18$

**Helping at Home**

After your child completes the page, ask him or her to explain patterns seen in the equations. Ask, "Why are all the numbers in order? Why do the numbers count down on the left side of the equations and up on the right?"

# Equations

An **equation** is like a balance scale. One side must be the same as the other side to be balanced, or equal. Add to or subtract from one side of the equation to make it true.

$$10 + 4 = 8 + 6$$

Add to or subtract from the right side of the equal sign to make the equation true.

1. $7 + 5 = 6$

2. $4 + 3 = 15$

3. $16 - 7 = 4$

4. $13 + 5 = 9$

5. $14 - 5 = 17$

6. $5 + 6 = 20$

Helping at Home
Write two math equations on two halves of a sheet of paper, then "tip" the paper in the direction of the equation with the answer that has the greater value. Invite your child to change one of the problems so that the two sides have equal values.

# Addition Strategies

Find the missing number in the problem.

| | | | |
|---|---|---|---|
| 1. | Paul's towel has 3 stripes. Mario's towel also has some stripes. There are 8 stripes in all. How many stripes does Mario's towel have?<br><br>$3 + \boxed{\phantom{0}} = 8$ stripes | 2. | Some sand dollars and 5 starfish were in a tidal pool. There were 11 animals in the tidal pool altogether. How many sand dollars were in the pool?<br><br>$\boxed{\phantom{0}} + 5 = 11$ animals |
| 3. | Liv has 7 diving rings and Rose also has some diving rings. Combined, they have 15 diving rings. How many diving rings does Rose have?<br><br>$7 + \boxed{\phantom{0}} = 15$ rings | 4. | The Samson family has 9 drinks in their cooler. The Stone family brings some more drinks to put in the cooler. There is now a total of 16 drinks in the cooler. How many drinks did the Stone family bring?<br><br>$9 + \boxed{\phantom{0}} = 16$ drinks |
| 5. | There are some seagulls on the beach. Four more seagulls flew down to join them. Now, there are 12 seagulls on the beach. How many seagulls flew down?<br><br>$\boxed{\phantom{0}} + 4 = 12$ seagulls | 6. | Fourteen children are building sand castles. Eight children are using shovels and the rest are using buckets. How many children are using buckets?<br><br>$8 + \boxed{\phantom{0}} = 14$ children |

© Carson-Dellosa • CD-734044

**Helping at Home**

On index cards, write numbers *1–20* and symbols + , -, and =. Cut the center from another card to make an empty frame. Decorate the frame. Then, form equations with the cards, putting the empty frame in various positions for your child to fill in.

# Subtraction Strategies

Add the bold number to the second number in each problem. If the sum is equal to the first number, the number sentence is true. If it is not equal, the number sentence is not true, or false.

Write *T* in the blank for the number sentences that are true for the bold number. Write *F* in the blank for the number sentences that are not true for the number.

1. **8**
15 – 7 = _____
14 – 9 = _____
14 – 6 = _____
18 – 10 = _____
17 – 4 = _____
17 – 9 = _____

2. **4**
18 – 4 = _____
13 – 9 = _____
15 – 8 = _____
12 – 8 = _____
9 – 5 = _____
14 – 0 = _____

3. **7**
9 – 2 = _____
10 – 4 = _____
11 – 4 = _____
12 – 5 = _____
20 – 10 = _____
15 – 8 = _____

4. **2**
8 – 6 = _____
16 – 9 = _____
12 – 10 = _____
14 – 8 = _____
9 – 7 = _____
7 – 6 = _____

5. **5**
14 – 9 = _____
15 – 0 = _____
13 – 8 = _____
11 – 6 = _____
17 – 9 = _____
15 – 10 = _____

6. **6**
17 – 9 = _____
10 – 2 = _____
12 – 6 = _____
15 – 9 = _____
18 – 8 = _____
14 – 8 = _____

**Helping at Home**
Draw an octopus shape with nine arms. Write a number, such as 6, on its head. On eight arms, write a problem whose answer is 6. On one arm, write a problem with a different answer. Can your child find the false number sentence and cross it out?

# Numbers and Number Words

Numbers can also be written as words.

**Examples:** 2 = two  8 = eight  11 = eleven  14 = fourteen

Write the number word of each clue to complete the puzzle. Use the word bank to the right for help.

**Across**

1.  15
2.  16
3.  12
5.  13
6.  20
7.  11
8.  19

**Down**

1.  14
2.  17
4.  18
6.  10

## Word Bank

| | |
|---|---|
| ten | sixteen |
| eleven | seventeen |
| twelve | eighteen |
| thirteen | nineteen |
| fourteen | twenty |
| fifteen | |

Make a piece of art with number words that have special meaning to your child, such as his or her age, birthdate, address, and classroom or bus number. Your child may wish to write each word in a different color or add illustrations.

# Numbers and Number Words

A **hyphen** (-) is used between number words with a tens name and a ones name.

**Examples:** forty-four = 44, sixty-four = 64

Write the number for each number word below. Cross out each slice of bread as the number written on it is used.

1. eighty-six    = _____       2. forty-nine    = _____

3. fifty-eight   = _____       4. fifty-six     = _____

5. forty-five    = _____       6. ninety-one    = _____

7. ninety-two    = _____       8. sixty-five    = _____

9. thirty-four   = _____       10. sixty-two    = _____

11. sixty-seven  = _____       12. eighty-four  = _____

13. thirteen     = _____       14. twenty-one   = _____

15. thirty       = _____       16. seventy-six  = _____

17. one hundred three  = _____

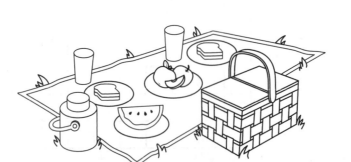

Helping at Home

Have your child write numbers *11–19* and number words *eleven–nineteen* on sheets of paper. Staple the pages together to make a book. On each page, ask your child to draw a picture of what he or she might be doing at that age.

# Numbers and Counting

Write the numbers on the lines to count the pieces of food.

___  ___  ___  ___  ___  ___  ___  ___  ___  ___

___  ___  ___  ___  ___  ___  ___  ___  ___  ___

___  ___  ___  ___  ___  ___  ___  ___  ___  ___

___  ___  ___  ___  ___  ___  ___  ___  ___  ___

___  ___  ___  ___  ___  ___  ___  ___  ___  ___

There are _____ pieces of fruit on the page.

**Helping at Home**

Have your child make a collection of 120 things on a poster board. It could be 120 little drawings, 120 stickers, or 120 glued-on things from nature. Count the items together, writing a number below each. Start from any number and count on.

# Numbers and Counting

Count by 1s. Write the missing numbers.

1.

| 51 | 52 | 53 |    |    |    | 57 |    | 59 |    |
|----|----|----|----|----|----|----|----|----|----|
|    | 62 |    | 64 | 65 |    |    | 68 |    | 70 |

2.

| 31 | 32 |    | 34 |    | 36 |    | 38 |    | 40 |
|----|----|----|----|----|----|----|----|----|----|
| 41 |    | 43 |    | 45 |    | 47 |    | 49 |    |

3.

| 71 |    |    |    | 75 | 76 | 77 |    |    | 80 |
|----|----|----|----|----|----|----|----|----|----|
|    | 82 | 83 | 84 |    |    |    |    | 89 |    |

4.

|     | 102 | 103 |     | 105 |     |     | 108 | 109 |     |
|-----|-----|-----|-----|-----|-----|-----|-----|-----|-----|
|     | 112 |     | 114 |     |     | 117 | 118 | 119 |     |

# Numbers and Counting

Write the number that comes before, between, or after each number listed.

| Before | | Between | | After | |
|---|---|---|---|---|---|
| ___ | 10 | 0 ___ | 2 | 90 | ___ |
| ___ | 6 | 25 ___ | 27 | 17 | ___ |
| ___ | 12 | 71 ___ | 73 | 29 | ___ |
| ___ | 21 | 19 ___ | 21 | 80 | ___ |
| ___ | 38 | 85 ___ | 87 | 18 | ___ |
| ___ | 14 | 49 ___ | 51 | 109 | ___ |
| ___ | 3 | 93 ___ | 95 | 39 | ___ |
| ___ | 67 | 99 ___ | 101 | 93 | ___ |
| ___ | 49 | 13 ___ | 15 | 21 | ___ |
| ___ | 8 | 58 ___ | 60 | 66 | ___ |
| ___ | 100 | 10 ___ | 12 | 15 | ___ |

**Helping at Home**

Ask your child to count all the numbers between his or her age and your age, all the numbers between the current page of this book and the end of this book, or all the numbers between today and a holiday.

# Place Value

To count large groups, it is easiest to make groups of 10. The number of groups is written in the tens place. The number of leftovers is written in the ones place.

**Example:**

1 group of 10          4 ones

| Tens | Ones |
|------|------|
| 1    |      |

| Tens | Ones |
|------|------|
| 1    | 4    |

Circle each group of 10. Then, write the total number of tens and ones.

1.

| Tens | Ones |
|------|------|
|      |      |

2.

| Tens | Ones |
|------|------|
|      |      |

3.

| Tens | Ones |
|------|------|
|      |      |

4.

| Tens | Ones |
|------|------|
|      |      |

5.

| Tens | Ones |
|------|------|
|      |      |

6.

| Tens | Ones |
|------|------|
|      |      |

Helping at Home

Play with one dime and nine pennies. Explain that each dime equals 10 pennies. Ask your child to show how many pennies must be added to the dime to make 14¢? 18¢? 12¢?

# Place Value

Imagine taking 10 small blocks and putting them together like this:

The block is now called a **tens rod**. Leftover blocks are called **ones blocks**.

Count the tens rods and ones blocks.

1.

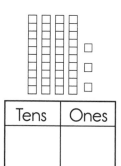

| Tens | Ones |
|------|------|
|      |      |

2.

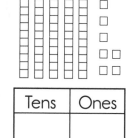

| Tens | Ones |
|------|------|
|      |      |

3.

| Tens | Ones |
|------|------|
|      |      |

4.

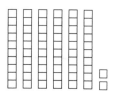

| Tens | Ones |
|------|------|
|      |      |

5.

| Tens | Ones |
|------|------|
|      |      |

6.

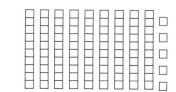

| Tens | Ones |
|------|------|
|      |      |

**Helping at Home**

Show your child how to use interlocking blocks to make stacks of 10. Then, call out a number such as *28* or *42*. Challenge your child to represent the number with stacks of ten blocks and single blocks.

# Place Value

Two-digit numbers have two parts: the tens column (place) and the ones column (place). The columns determine a digit's place value. Numbers can also be shown using tens rods and ones blocks.

**Example:**

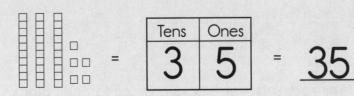

| Tens | Ones |
|------|------|
| 3 | 5 |

= 35

Draw a picture of the tens rods and ones blocks to show each number. Write the number.

1.
=
| Tens | Ones |
|------|------|
| 6 | 3 |
= _____

2.
=
| Tens | Ones |
|------|------|
| 7 | 8 |
= _____

3.
=
| Tens | Ones |
|------|------|
| 5 | 1 |
= _____

4.
=
| Tens | Ones |
|------|------|
| 0 | 2 |
= _____

5.
=
| Tens | Ones |
|------|------|
| 0 | 9 |
= _____

6.
=
| Tens | Ones |
|------|------|
| 1 | 9 |
= _____

**Helping at Home** Cut long strips of paper and have your child snip them into many small squares. Then, give a two-digit number such as *33*. Provide a large sheet of paper and ask your child to glue the squares into tens stacks and ones to show the number.

# Place Value

Write how many tens and ones. Then, write the total.

1.

_____ tens _____ ones = _____ total

2.

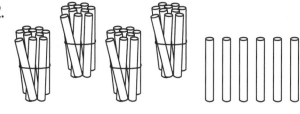

_____ tens _____ ones = _____ total

3.

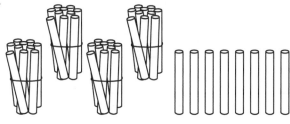

_____ tens _____ ones = _____ total

4.

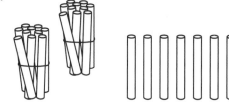

_____ tens _____ ones = _____ total

5.

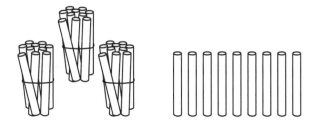

_____ tens _____ ones = _____ total

6.

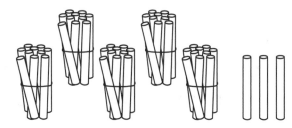

_____ tens _____ ones = _____ total

**Helping at Home**

Provide a box of 100 paper clips and have your child build nine chains of 10, leaving the last 10 paper clips loose. Then, call out two-digit numbers such as *26*, *61*, and *99*. Challenge your child to represent the numbers with the paper clips.

# Place Value

Think about the number of tens in the numbers in each row and the number of ones in the numbers in each column. Think about the last row by itself. Answer the questions.

| 1 | 2 | 3 | 4 | 5 | 6 | 7 | 8 | 9 | 10 |
|---|---|---|---|---|---|---|---|---|----|
| 11 | 12 | 13 | 14 | 15 | 16 | 17 | 18 | 19 | 20 |
| 21 | 22 | 23 | 24 | 25 | 26 | 27 | 28 | 29 | 30 |
| 31 | 32 | 33 | 34 | 35 | 36 | 37 | 38 | 39 | 40 |
| 41 | 42 | 43 | 44 | 45 | 46 | 47 | 48 | 49 | 50 |
| 51 | 52 | 53 | 54 | 55 | 56 | 57 | 58 | 59 | 60 |
| 61 | 62 | 63 | 64 | 65 | 66 | 67 | 68 | 69 | 70 |
| 71 | 72 | 73 | 74 | 75 | 76 | 77 | 78 | 79 | 80 |
| 81 | 82 | 83 | 84 | 85 | 86 | 87 | 88 | 89 | 90 |
| 91 | 92 | 93 | 94 | 95 | 96 | 97 | 98 | 99 | 100 |

1. What numbers have 4 ones? _____

2. What numbers have 7 tens?_____

3. What numbers have no ones? _____

4. What numbers have no tens? _____

5. What numbers have 6 tens? _____

6. What numbers have 6 ones?_____

7. What numbers have 7 ones? _____

8. What number(s) have 3 tens and 5 ones? _____

Give clues to a two-digit number. Clues may include addition or subtraction problems that equal the number, numbers that come before or after, number of tens, and number of ones. Can your child guess the number?

# Comparing Numbers

Write the numbers for the pictures and compare them using > or <.

1.
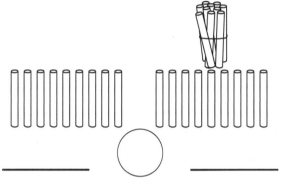

_____   ◯   _____

2.
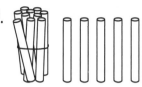 

_____   ◯   _____

3.
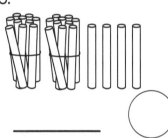 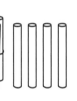 

_____   ◯   _____

4.

_____   ◯   _____

5.
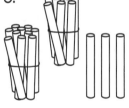 

_____   ◯   _____

6.
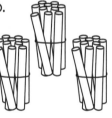 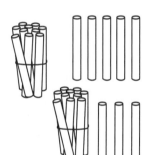

_____   ◯   _____

Circle the one that is greater.

7.   2 tens, 7 ones
     7 tens, 2 ones

8.   6 tens, 9 ones
     9 tens, 6 ones

9.   9 tens, 9 ones
     9 tens, 8 ones

10.  4 tens, 8 ones
     8 tens, 4 ones

11.  5 tens, 3 ones
     3 tens, 9 ones

12.  3 tens, 7 ones
     4 tens, 7 ones

**Helping at Home**

Use interlocking blocks to make stacks of 10. Use the ten-stacks along with single blocks to represent two, two-digit numbers. Then, invite your child to use a toy vehicle to knock down the blocks for the number that is less.

# Comparing Numbers

To compare two-digit numbers, follow these steps:

1. Look at the tens place. The larger digit is greater.

   Example: 7̲2 > 3̲9

2. If the tens are the same, look at the ones place.

   Example: 3̲4̲ < 3̲8̲

Remember: < means *less than*, and > means *greater than*.

Write >, <, or = to compare each set of numbers.

1. 19 ◯ 31

2. 23 ◯ 17

3. 40 ◯ 20

4. 78 ◯ 78

5. 84 ◯ 49

6. 38 ◯ 32

7. 76 ◯ 77

8. 73 ◯ 37

9. 57 ◯ 66

10. 61 ◯ 64

**Helping at Home** Call out a two-digit number and then say, "greater" or "lesser." Can your child quickly name a number that fits? Take turns giving numbers and see how quickly you can go. The first one to make a mistake is out.

# Adding Two-Digit Numbers

When you add 2-digit numbers, add the ones first and then add the tens. Remember that when you are adding the tens, you are not adding 3 and 2, but 3 tens and 2 tens, or 30 and 20.

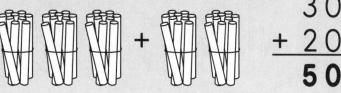

$$
\begin{array}{r}
30 \\
+\ 20 \\
\hline
\mathbf{50}
\end{array}
$$

Add to solve each problem.

1.  
$$\begin{array}{r} 20 \\ +\ 40 \\ \hline \end{array}$$
$$\begin{array}{r} 50 \\ +\ 10 \\ \hline \end{array}$$
$$\begin{array}{r} 70 \\ +\ 20 \\ \hline \end{array}$$
$$\begin{array}{r} 30 \\ +\ 40 \\ \hline \end{array}$$
$$\begin{array}{r} 60 \\ +\ 20 \\ \hline \end{array}$$

2.  
$$\begin{array}{r} 10 \\ +\ 80 \\ \hline \end{array}$$
$$\begin{array}{r} 20 \\ +\ 50 \\ \hline \end{array}$$
$$\begin{array}{r} 30 \\ +\ 30 \\ \hline \end{array}$$
$$\begin{array}{r} 70 \\ +\ 10 \\ \hline \end{array}$$
$$\begin{array}{r} 50 \\ +\ 40 \\ \hline \end{array}$$

3.  
$$\begin{array}{r} 71 \\ +\ 10 \\ \hline \end{array}$$
$$\begin{array}{r} 54 \\ +\ 10 \\ \hline \end{array}$$
$$\begin{array}{r} 43 \\ +\ 10 \\ \hline \end{array}$$
$$\begin{array}{r} 36 \\ +\ 10 \\ \hline \end{array}$$
$$\begin{array}{r} 27 \\ +\ 10 \\ \hline \end{array}$$

4. Explain how you solved the problems in row 3. _____

_____

© Carson-Dellosa • CD-734044

**Helping at Home**

Provide dimes and pennies and ask your child to use them to illustrate several problems from this page. Remind your child that a dime equals 10 pennies, or 10 ones. How many cents does each problem add up to?

# Subtracting Two-Digit Numbers

Just like with addition, you start with the ones when subtracting 2-digit numbers. Remember to think about 7 tens as 70, not 7!

$$
\begin{array}{r}
70 \\
-\ 40 \\
\hline
\mathbf{30}
\end{array}
$$

Subtract to solve each problem.

1.
$$
\begin{array}{r} 60 \\ -\ 20 \\ \hline \end{array}
\qquad
\begin{array}{r} 50 \\ -\ 10 \\ \hline \end{array}
\qquad
\begin{array}{r} 80 \\ -\ 50 \\ \hline \end{array}
\qquad
\begin{array}{r} 70 \\ -\ 20 \\ \hline \end{array}
\qquad
\begin{array}{r} 40 \\ -\ 30 \\ \hline \end{array}
$$

2.
$$
\begin{array}{r} 70 \\ -\ 30 \\ \hline \end{array}
\qquad
\begin{array}{r} 50 \\ -\ 20 \\ \hline \end{array}
\qquad
\begin{array}{r} 60 \\ -\ 50 \\ \hline \end{array}
\qquad
\begin{array}{r} 80 \\ -\ 40 \\ \hline \end{array}
\qquad
\begin{array}{r} 40 \\ -\ 20 \\ \hline \end{array}
$$

3.
$$
\begin{array}{r} 56 \\ -\ 10 \\ \hline \end{array}
\qquad
\begin{array}{r} 67 \\ -\ 10 \\ \hline \end{array}
\qquad
\begin{array}{r} 84 \\ -\ 10 \\ \hline \end{array}
\qquad
\begin{array}{r} 97 \\ -\ 10 \\ \hline \end{array}
\qquad
\begin{array}{r} 38 \\ -\ 10 \\ \hline \end{array}
$$

4. Explain how you solved the problems in row 3. _____

_____

Practice counting backward by tens with your child. Then, give directions for solving one of the problems on this page. For example, for the first problem, say, "Start at 60. Count backward two tens." Have your child give you directions, too.

**Helping at Home**

# Adding and Subtracting 10

Draw a picture or write to explain how to find 10 more and 10 less than a number.

1. How can you use a number line to find the answer to 48 – 10?

2. How can you use a hundreds board, like the one on page 98, to find the answer to 61 + 10?

3. How can you model 51 – 10 using tens rods and ones blocks?

4. How can knowing how to find 10 less help you find the answer to 87 – 30?

**Helping at Home**

Ask your child which method for adding and subtracting 10 described on this page is easiest to use and understand. Encourage your child to explain his or her answer and to give an example. Praise your child by saying, "You are good at math!"

# Addition with Regrouping

Look at the example of regrouping below: 10 ones are regrouped to be 1 ten. The total number of blocks does not change. The number of tens and ones does. Regrouping is needed when adding if the sum of the ones column is 10 or more.

| | T | O |
|---|---|---|
| | 0 | 16 |

16 ones

| | T | O |
|---|---|---|
| | 1 | |
| | 0 | 6 |
| | 1 | 6 |

1 tens    6 ones

Regroup. Use the tens and ones columns to write each number.

1.
| T | O |
|---|---|
| □ | |

12 ones

2.
| T | O |
|---|---|
| □ | |

13 ones

3.
| T | O |
|---|---|
| □ | |

18 ones

4.
| T | O |
|---|---|
| □ | |

17 ones

Add the ones. Use the blocks to help you regroup the ones and add to the tens.

5.
| T | O |
|---|---|
| □ | |
| 1 | 7 |
| + | 5 |

6.
| T | O |
|---|---|
| □ | |
| 1 | 5 |
| + | 6 |

**Helping at Home** Think aloud as you help your child solve an addition problem with regrouping. Encourage your child to talk it through, too. Explain that only ones will fit in the ones column or "ones house." A ten spills over to the "tens house" next door.

# Addition with Regrouping

Sometimes when adding, the sum of the ones column is 10 or more. When this happens, **regroup** 10 ones as 1 ten and add it to the tens column. Leave the leftover ones in the ones column.

1. Add the ones. Carry the 1 ten over to the tens column.

$$
\begin{array}{r}
\overset{1}{\phantom{0}} \\
2\,8 \\
+\,4\,5 \\
\hline
3
\end{array}
$$

8 + 5 = 13 ones

13 ones = 1 ten 3 ones

2. Add the tens.

$$
\begin{array}{r}
\overset{1}{\phantom{0}} \\
2\,8 \\
+\,4\,5 \\
\hline
7\,3
\end{array}
$$

Add. Regroup the ones.

1. 
$$
\begin{array}{r}
64 \\
+\ 8 \\
\hline
\end{array}
$$

2. 
$$
\begin{array}{r}
76 \\
+\ 5 \\
\hline
\end{array}
$$

3. 
$$
\begin{array}{r}
29 \\
+\ 2 \\
\hline
\end{array}
$$

4. 
$$
\begin{array}{r}
63 \\
+\ 9 \\
\hline
\end{array}
$$

5. 
$$
\begin{array}{r}
35 \\
+\ 6 \\
\hline
\end{array}
$$

6. 
$$
\begin{array}{r}
47 \\
+\ 8 \\
\hline
\end{array}
$$

7. 
$$
\begin{array}{r}
26 \\
+\ 6 \\
\hline
\end{array}
$$

8. 
$$
\begin{array}{r}
17 \\
+\ 5 \\
\hline
\end{array}
$$

9. 
$$
\begin{array}{r}
43 \\
+\ 7 \\
\hline
\end{array}
$$

10. 
$$
\begin{array}{r}
55 \\
+\ 5 \\
\hline
\end{array}
$$

11. 
$$
\begin{array}{r}
35 \\
+\ 9 \\
\hline
\end{array}
$$

12. 
$$
\begin{array}{r}
49 \\
+\ 9 \\
\hline
\end{array}
$$

**Helping at Home**

Work with your child to solve the problems *11 + 8* and *11+ 9*. Talk about why regrouping must be used to solve the second problem. What is different about the two answers, *19* and *20*? How many tens does each number have?

# Comparing Lengths

Order the objects from shortest to longest (1–3).

1. 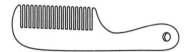  _____

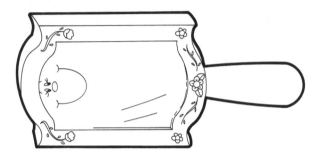  _____

  _____

2.

_____    _____    _____

© Carson-Dellosa • CD-734044

Helping at Home

Cut a piece of yarn or string to match your child's height. Encourage your child to go around the house, using the string to find things that are taller or shorter than his or her height.

# Measuring with Units

The ambulance is 8 units long.

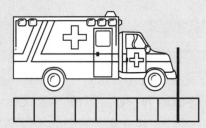

Write how many units long each object is.

1.

☐☐☐☐☐☐☐☐☐☐☐☐

_____

2.

☐☐☐☐☐☐☐☐☐☐☐☐

_____

3.

☐☐☐☐☐☐☐☐☐☐☐☐

_____

4.

☐☐☐☐☐☐☐☐☐☐☐☐

_____

5.

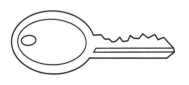

☐☐☐☐☐☐☐☐☐☐☐☐

_____

6.

 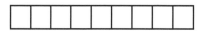

☐☐☐☐☐☐☐☐☐☐☐☐

_____

**Helping at Home**

Choose a unit such as a large paper clip, a block, or a short piece of yarn. Ask your child to use the unit to measure the length of several small objects around the house such as a book or a shoe. How many units long was each item?

# Measurement Problems

Think about measurement to answer each question.

1. Connor and Julio each made a candy train. They laid candy end-to-end on the table. Connor used all chocolate bars. Julio used all mints. Connor's train was 8 candies long. Julio's train was 12 candies long. Julio thought his train was longer because he used more candies. Is he right? Why or why not?

_____

_____

2. Three friends compared how tall they are. Sasha is taller than Lynn but shorter than Dawn. Write the friends' names in order from tallest to shortest.

_____     _____     _____

3. Lucy and her little brother, Tyler, measured the length of their bedrooms. They used their feet to measure. Lucy put her feet toe-to-heel across the room. Tyler took normal steps across his room. Who measured the best way? Why?

_____

_____

4. If Lucy measured Tyler's room, would she get the same measurement that Tyler got for his room? Why or why not?

_____

_____

Choose two units such as the length of your child's hand and a shorter length of yarn. Measure a tabletop twice, once with each unit, and record the results. Which measurement is correct? Help your child understand that both are valid.

Helping at Home

# Telling Time

The short hand on a clock is the **hour hand**. The numbers around the clock tell the hour. At the exact hour, the hour hand will point directly to the number of the hour. At the half hour, the hour hand will point halfway between numbers. The hour stays the same until the hour hand reaches the next hour.

The long hand on a clock is called the **minute hand**. When the minute hand is on the 12, it is 0 minutes past the hour. When the minute hand is on the 6, it is 30 minutes past the hour.

In the first example, the hour hand is pointing to the 8 and the minute hand is pointing to the 12, so it is 8:00. In the second example, the hour hand is halfway between the 8 and the 9 and the minute hand is pointing to the 6, so it is 8:30.

8:00          8:30

Write the time shown on each clock.

1.

_____

2.

_____

3.

_____

4.

_____

5.

_____

6.

_____

© Carson-Dellosa • CD-734044

**Helping at Home**

Look at the time your child wrote for each clock. Ask your child to think about what he or she is usually doing at about that time of day. Work together to draw new clocks that show what time school starts and what time it ends each day.

# Telling Time

Time can be named in many ways.

 8:30, or
half past 8:00

 8:00, or
8 o'clock

Circle the correct time below each clock.

1.

A.   10 o'clock

B.   9 o'clock

C.   11 o'clock

2.

A.   11 o'clock

B.   12 o'clock

C.   1 o'clock

3.

A.   half past 9:00

B.   half past 8:00

C.   half past 10:00

4.

A.   half past 2:00

B.   half past 3:00

C.   half past 4:00

5.

A.   half past 6:00

B.   half past 9:00

C.   half past 10:00

6.

A.   6 o'clock

B.   2 o'clock

C.   half past 12:00

**Helping at Home**

Draw a clock face that shows the long hand at either the 12 or 6 position. Ask your child to tell whether the clock will show a time that ends in :00 or :30. Then, have your child draw in the hour hand at any position and tell the complete time.

# Telling Time

Match each clock on the left to the digital clock on the right with the same time.

1.

A.

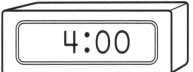

2.

B.

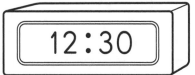

3.

C.

4.

D.

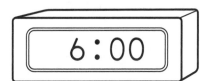

5.

E.

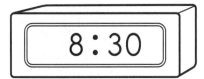

**Helping at Home**

Work with your child to make a clock face using a paper plate, a paper fastener, and construction paper hands. Practice using the clock to tell time. When your child sees a digital clock, challenge him or her to show the same time on the clock face.

# Counting Data

Samaria was counting the animals on the farm. She saw pigs, sheep, and cows. She put an **X** under each animal name as she counted.

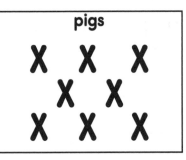

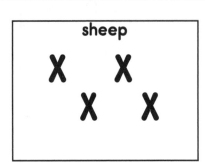

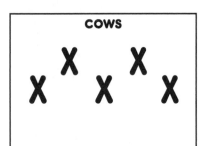

Use the data to answer each question.

1.  How many cows are on the farm? _____ cows

2.  How many pigs are on the farm? _____ pigs

3.  How many more cows are there than sheep on the farm? _____ more cow(s)

4.  How many fewer sheep than pigs are there on the farm? _____ fewer sheep

5.  How many animals are on the farm altogether? _____ animals

6.  Which type of animal are there the most of on the farm? _____

© Carson-Dellosa • CD-734044

**Helping at Home**

Make a box for each hair color represented in your child's classroom. Have your child put an X in the box for each child with that hair color. Make observations about the results. Which color is most common? Least common?

# Counting Data

## Frogs in Raul's Pond

|  | Monday | Tuesday | Wednesday |
|---|---|---|---|
| Frogs | 7 | 5 | 4 |

Use the data to answer each question.

1. How many frogs were in the pond on Wednesday? _____

2. On which day were the most frogs in the pond? _____

3. On which day were there 4 frogs in the pond? _____

4. How many total frogs were in the pond on all 3 days? _____

5. On which day were there the fewest frogs in the pond? _____

6. How many more frogs were in the pond on Monday than on Tuesday? _____

Help your child keep track of how many hours he or she sleeps each night for one week. Record the data in a chart like the one at the top of this page. Ask your child to use the data to write three questions for you to answer.

# Counting Data

Color all of the triangles orange. Color all of the rectangles red. Color all of the squares brown. Then, answer the questions below.

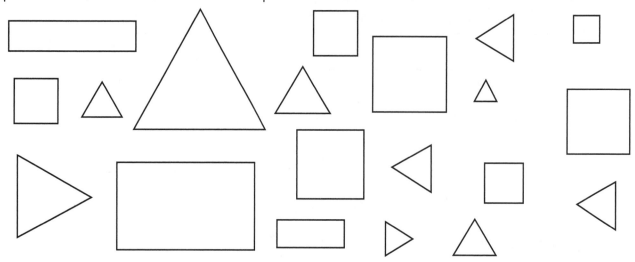

1. Write how many there are of each shape.

   _____ squares        _____ triangles        _____ rectangles

2. How many shapes are there in all? _____

3. How many more triangles than rectangles are there? _____

4. How many fewer rectangles are there than squares? _____

5. Squares are a type of rectangle. If you counted all of the squares as rectangles, would there be more rectangles or triangles? Explain.

   _____

6. Write a question you could ask about the data.

   _____

   _____

# Shapes

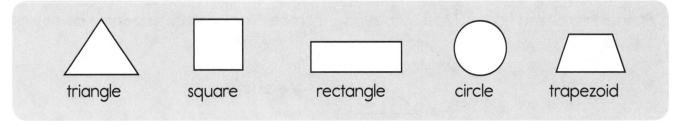

triangle    square    rectangle    circle    trapezoid

Count the hidden shapes in the picture below. Then, complete the chart.

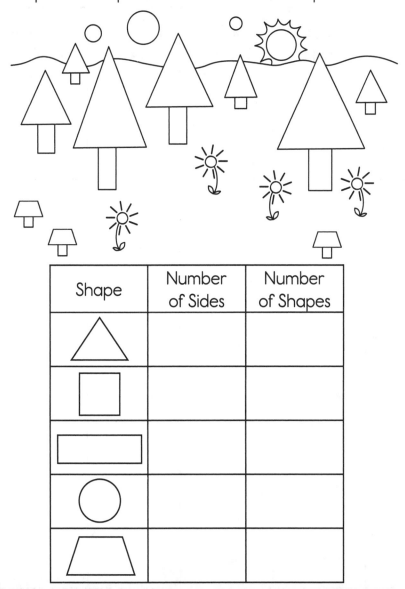

| Shape | Number of Sides | Number of Shapes |
|-------|-----------------|------------------|
| ▲ |  |  |
| ◻ |  |  |
| ▬ |  |  |
| ● |  |  |
| ⏢ |  |  |

Helping at Home

Look at the shapes at the top of this page with your child. Give clues to one of the shapes. For example, for a square, say, "This shape has four sides and four corners. All the sides are the same length. What is it?" Have your child give clues, too.

# Shapes

Shapes are closed figures. Most shapes have corners, sides, and angles. Some do not.

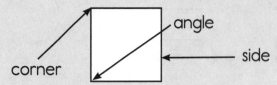

Complete the chart. Use the figures to the right for help.

| Shape Name | Draw the Shape | Number of Corners | Number of Sides | Number of Angles |
|---|---|---|---|---|
| 1. trapezoid | | | | |
| 2. circle | | | | |
| 3. triangle | | | | |
| 4. square | | | | |
| 5. rectangle | | | | |

**Helping at Home** As you are driving in the car, encourage your child to look for road signs that are shaped like triangles, squares, rectangles, circles, and trapezoids. Call out shapes when you see them. Have your child keep a tally. Which shape is most common?

# Composite Shapes

Tell what shapes are needed to make each figure.

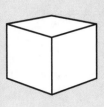
cube

cone

cylinder

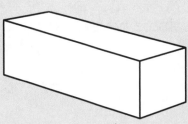
rectangular prism

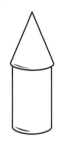

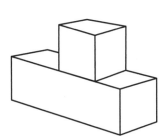

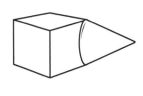

1. _____

2. _____

3. _____

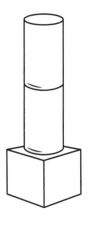

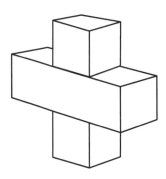

4. _____

5. _____

6. _____

**Helping at Home**

Encourage your child to color each solid figure on this page a different color. For example, color all the cubes red. Look around for examples of solid shapes. You may find a table leg that is a rectangular prism or a cereal box that is a cylinder.

# Equal Parts

When shapes are divided into equal parts or shares, each part is exactly the same.

These have equal parts:

These do not have equal parts:

Color the shapes that show equal parts.

1.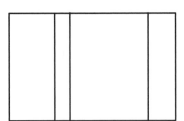

2.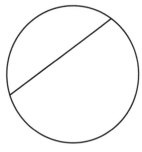

3.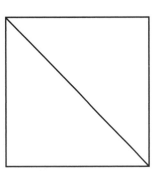

4.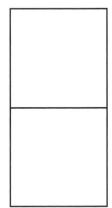

5.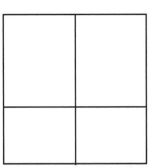

6.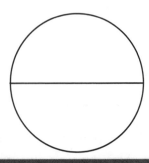

**Helping at Home**

Assemble snack ingredients that can be easily cut with a plastic knife. You might use slices of bread, apple, banana, or cheese. Take turns with your child dividing each piece of food into parts. Are the shares equal or not?

# Halves

A whole can be divided into 2 equal parts or shares. The apple on the left is cut into 2 equal parts. The parts are called **halves**. The parts of the apple on the right are not equal. The parts are not halves.

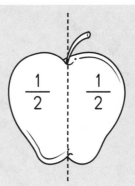 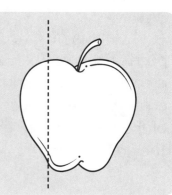

Color each food that shows 2 equal shares, or halves.

1.

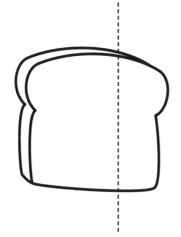

2.

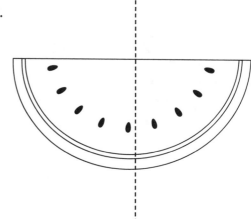

3.

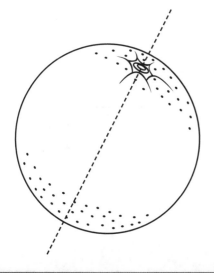

4.

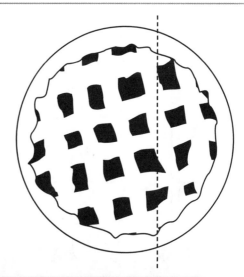

# Fourths

A whole can be divided into 4 equal parts or shares. The pizza on the left is cut into 4 equal parts. The parts are called **fourths** or quarters. The parts of the pizza on the right are not equal. They are not fourths.

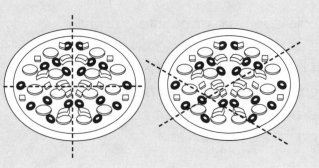

Color each food that shows 4 equal shares.

1.

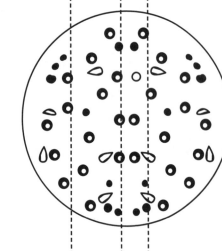

2.

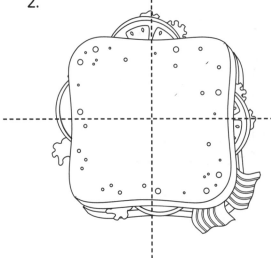

3.

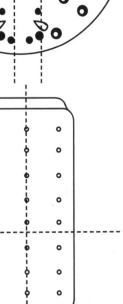

4.

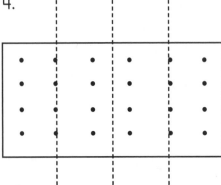

© Carson-Dellosa • CD-734044

**Helping at Home**

When your child plays with modeling dough, ask him or her to run a pretend pizza shop. Phone in orders for pizzas and specify whether they should be cut into halves or fourths. The shop might offer rectangular and circular pizza varieties.

# Fourths and Halves

Draw lines to divide shapes into halves in different ways.

1.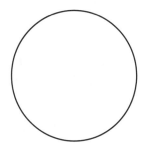

2.

3.

4.

5.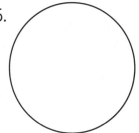

6.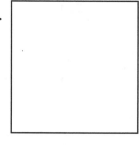

Draw lines to divide shapes into fourths, or quarters, in different ways.

7.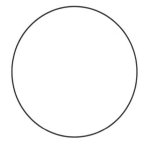

8.

9.

10.

11.

12.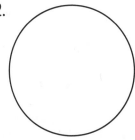

**Helping at Home**

Provide construction paper circles and rectangles and invite your child to cut them into halves and fourths in different ways. Encourage your child to play with the pieces and reassemble the shapes. Ask, "How many fourths make a half?"

# Answer Key

**Page 10**
1. C; 2. A; 3. A

**Page 11**
1. C; 2. B; 3. Answers will vary. 4. Answers will vary.

**Page 12**
1. Billy and Katie decide to do nothing. Setting drawings may include an apple tree.

**Page 13**
1. Answers will vary but may include I love spring, I like to sing, I wish I were a bird, or I feel like a king. 2. Answers will vary. 3. Answers will vary.

**Page 14**
1. Fact; 2. Story; 3. Fact; 4. Fact; 5. Story; 6. Answers will vary. 7. Answers will vary. 8. Answers will vary.

**Page 15**
1. Sammy Snail, Robby Rabbit, Kami Kangaroo; 2. Robby Rabbit; 3. Kami Kangaroo; 4. Answers will vary but should not be any of the quotes.

**Page 16**
2. Answers will vary. 3. Ruby, Judy, Hugo, Luke, Susan, June, Duke; 4. It takes place at the music show. 5. Ruby and her friends put on a music show.

**Page 17**
Vine Mouse: lived under a vine outside a large house, liked to eat plain rice, liked to play hide-and-seek outside. Tile Mouse: lived under the tiles inside the large house, liked to eat bites of fine food, liked to sit inside.

**Page 18**
1. banana; 2. jelly; 3. wings; 4. sausage; 5. eyes

**Page 19**
1. What is the Dead Sea? 2. The Salty Waters of the Dead Sea; 3. The Uses of the Dead Sea; 4. The Water Cycle of the Dead Sea

**Page 20**
1. Hoard means to keep or store. 2. Nocturnal means to be up at night. 3. To stay up very late is to be awake in the nighttime. 4. Answers will vary.

**Page 21**
1. Elena; 2. Math; 3. Monday; 4. Listening; 5. Sam; 6. Friday

**Page 22**
Flag answers will vary based on student perception of flags (colors, symbols) and research. Flag color words include: red, white, blue for the American flag; red and white for the Canadian flag; and red, white, and green for the Mexican flag.

**Page 23**
1. 8; 2. 2; 3. Mrs. Lopez's First-Grade Class: Ways to Get Home; 4. bus

**Page 25**
Similar: Both stories are about lies and what can happen when a person lies. Different: Mamad always told the truth, and Pinocchio lied. Mamad is in Africa, and Pinocchio is in Italy. 1. The king learned Mamad is honest and wise. 2. Pinocchio learned it is bad to lie. 3. Answers will vary.

# Answer Key

**Page 26**
1. It is sweet, and it cools the author down on a hot day. 2. They are fun to build at the beach and with friends.

**Page 27**
1. yes; 2. no; 3. yes; 4. no; 5. yes; 6. no; 7. no; 8. Answers will vary.

**Page 28**
Answers will vary but may include:
rat: bat, cat, fat, hat, mat, Nat, pat, sat
Tim: him, Jim, Kim, rim, swim, whim
kit: bit, fit, hit, lit, mitt, sit, wit
rate: bate, date, fate, gate, late, Kate, Nate
time: dime, grime, lime, mime, rhyme
kite: bite, mite, quite, site, white, write

**Page 29**

| Word | Beginning Sound | Middle Sound | Ending Sound |
|------|-----------------|--------------|--------------|
| bun | b | u | n |
| hip | h | i | p |
| get | g | e | t |
| sun | s | u | n |
| bat | b | a | t |

| Word | Beginning Sound 1 | Beginning Sound 2 | Middle Sound | Ending Sound |
|------|-------------------|-------------------|--------------|--------------|
| flip | f | l | i | p |
| brim | b | r | i | m |
| swap | s | w | a | p |
| slim | s | l | i | m |
| grip | g | r | i | p |

**Page 30**
1. f; 2. o; 3. t; 4. w; 5. e; 6. d; 7. g; 8. a; 9. t; 10. k; 11. Answers will vary.

**Page 31**
1. d; 2. p; 3. m; 4. p; 5. a; 6. u; 7. a; 8. e; 9. g; 10. t; 11. n; 12. t

**Page 32**
1. tr; 2. sl; 3. cl; 4. sn; 5. ch; 6. sh; 7. sh; 8. th

**Page 33**
Answers will vary.

**Page 34**
1. 2; 2. 1; 3. 1; 4. 2; 5. 3; 6. 4; 7. 3; 8. 2; 9. 5; 10. 2; 11. hippopotamus; 12. 2; 13. yard; 14. 4

**Page 35**
1. ape; 2. bone; 3. kite; 4. joke; 5. tube; 6. plate; 7. brave; 8. prize

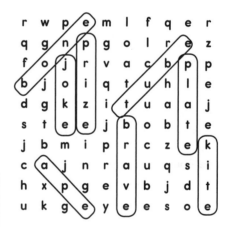

**Page 36**
1. sleep; 2. rain; 3. soap; 4. pail; 5. boat; 6. beach; 7. see

**Page 37**
1. railroad; 2. drumstick; 3. soapsuds 4. airplane; 5. seashell; 6. football; 7. fireworks; 8. playhouse

**Page 38**
1. pulled; 2. picked; 3. asked; 4. wanted; 5. looked; 6. helped;

# Answer Key

7. turned; 8. climbed; 9. Answers will vary. 10. Answers will vary.

**Page 39**
1. talking; 2. sleeping;
3. watching; 4. cooking;
5. crying; 6. cleaning;
7. jumping; 8. mixing; 9. Answers will vary. 10. Answers will vary.

**Page 40**
Answers will vary.

**Page 41**
Answers will vary.

**Page 42**
Answers will vary.

**Page 43**
Answers will vary.

**Page 44**
Answers will vary.

**Page 45**
Answers will vary.

**Page 46**
Answers will vary.

**Page 47**
Answers will vary.

**Page 48**
Answers will vary.

**Page 49**
Common Nouns
Person: dad, mother
Place: bedroom, school
Thing: chair, swing
Idea: love, freedom
Proper Nouns
Person: Mrs. Wu, Casey
Place: America, Florida

Thing: Friday, January

**Page 50**
Uppercase and lowercase letters should be in appropriate tables.
1. are; 2. wants; 3. writes; 4. eat; 5. is

**Page 51**
1. furry; 2. loud; 3. round; 4. bumpy;
5. tough; 6. sandy; 7. soft; 8. sweet

**Page 52**
1. or; 2. but; 3. and; 4. but; 5. or;
6. but; 7. and; 8. and

**Page 53**
1. an; 2. a; 3. a; 4. a; 5. an; 6. a;
7. an; 8. a; 9. a; 10. a

**Page 54**
1. in; 2. on; 3. at; 4. behind;
5. around; 6. across; 7. over;
8. inside; 9. down

**Page 55**
1. A; 2. E; 3. A; 4. T; 5. E; 6. C; 7. T; 8. A; 9. T; 10. C

**Page 56**
1. We; 2. She; 3. He; 4. It;
5. They 6. Elias was going to the store. 7. Henry felt very happy.
8. Would you take me to the lake?

**Page 57**
1. eggs, flour, and butter; 2. salad, pears, and bread;  3. Joannie, Grace, and Sam;  4. yellow, black, and gray; 5. turkey, tomato, and lettuce; 6. games, puzzles, and cards; 7. lions, elephants, and tigers;
8. balloons, cake, and streamers;
9. February 4, 2010; 10. November 12, 2014

© Carson-Dellosa • CD-734044

# Answer Key

## Page 58
1. Preview: to look before, or Review: to look again; 2. Untie: to take ties apart; 3. Retake: to take again; 4. Restless: to be without rest, or Restful: to be full of rest; 5. Helpful: to be full of help, or Helpless: without help; 6. Buildable: able to be built

## Page 59
Fruits We Eat: apple, banana, orange, pear
Things We Wear: coat, glove, hat, scarf
Things We Eat with: bowl, dish, fork, spoon

## Page 60
Birds that Swim: duck, goose, penguin, swan
Large Cats: bobcat, jaguar, lion, tiger
Green Reptiles: iguana, lizard, snake, turtle

## Page 61
Green Vegetables: broccoli, cucumber, lettuce, peas
Things with Wheels: bike, car, skateboard, tricycle
Ice-Cream Flavors: chocolate, mint, strawberry, vanilla

## Page 63
Answers will vary.

## Page 68
1. $4 + 1 = 5$; 2. $1 + 1 = 2$; 3. $3 + 3 = 6$; 4. $4 + 2 = 6$; 5. $4 + 5 = 9$; 6. $1 + 3 = 4$

## Page 69
1. 4; 2. 6; 3. 4; 4. 5

## Page 70
1. 1; 2. 2; 3. 1; 4. 4; 5. 3; 6. 5

## Page 71
1. total, $6 + 2 = 8$ crayons; 2. combined, $8 + 7 = 15$ pencils; 3. altogether, $5 + 3 = 8$ paper clips; 4. in all, $5 + 2 + 1 = 8$ pens; 5. total, $7 + 2 = 9$ erasers; 6. in all, $3 + 4 + 3 = 10$ markers

## Page 72
1. $3 + 4 + 5 = 12$ carrots; 2. $6 + 7 = 13$ pencils; 3. $5 + 9 = 14$ fish; 4. $2 + 8 + 3 = 13$ cans of paint; 5. $5 + 4 + 8 = 17$ miles; 6. $8 + 7 = 15$ butterflies

## Page 73
1. $3 + 1 = 4$, $1 + 3 = 4$, $4 - 1 = 3$, $4 - 3 = 1$; 2. $2 + 3 = 5$, $3 + 2 = 5$, $5 - 2 = 3$, $5 - 3 = 2$; 3. $1 + 2 = 3$, $2 + 1 = 3$, $3 - 1 = 2$, $3 - 2 = 1$; 4. $2 + 4 = 6$, $4 + 2 = 6$, $6 - 2 = 4$, $6 - 4 = 2$

## Page 74
1. $3 + 7 = 10$, $7 + 3 = 10$, $10 - 3 = 7$, $10 - 7 = 3$; 2. $4 + 8 = 12$, $8 + 4 = 12$, $12 - 4 = 8$, $12 - 8 = 4$; 3. $4 + 9 = 13$, $9 + 4 = 13$, $13 - 4 = 9$, $13 - 9 = 4$; 4. $6 + 5 = 11$, $5 + 6 = 11$, $11 - 5 = 6$, $11 - 6 = 5$; 5. $5 + 8 = 13$, $8 + 5 = 13$, $13 - 5 = 8$, $13 - 8 = 5$; 6. $4 + 7 = 11$, $7 + 4 = 11$, $11 - 4 = 7$, $11 - 7 = 4$

## Page 75
1. 4; 2. 4; 3. 4; 4. 4; 5. 6; 6. 2

## Page 76
1. $7 - 4 = 3$ coins; 2. $9 - 2 = 7$ candies; 3. $11 - 5 = 6$ books;

# Answer Key

4. 8 – 3 = 5 fish;
5. 10 – 5 = 5 shells;
6. 12 – 3 = 9 eggs

**Page 77**
1. 15 + 2 = 17; 2. 9 + 3 = 12;
3. 11 + 5 = 16; 4. 8 + 6 = 14;
5. 14 + 6 = 20; 6. 8 + 3 = 11;
7. 9 + 4 = 13; 8. 12 + 7 = 19;
9. 10 + 8 = 18; 10. 11 + 4 = 15

**Page 78**
1. 7; 2. 9; 3. 7; 4. 8; 5. 9; 6. 7;
7. 9; 8. 8; 9. 5; 10. 7; 11. 6; 12. 8

**Page 79**
1. 6; 2. 12; 3. 10;
4. 4 + 4 + 1 = 9;
5. 6 + 6 + 1 = 13;
6. 7 + 7 = 14; 7. 7 + 7 + 1 = 15

**Page 80**
1. 10 + 5 = 15; 2. 10 + 1 = 11;
3. 10 + 1 = 11; 4. 10 + 7 = 17;
5. 10 + 4 = 14; 6. 10 + 2 = 12

**Page 81**
1. 12; 2. 12; 3. 15; 4. 12; 5. 14;
6. 16; 7. 17; 8. 18

**Page 82**
1. 9, 7, 11; 2. 2, 0, 8, 3, 5, 1;
3. 6, 8, 5, 7, 12, 13; 4. 0, 2, 3,
9, 4, 1; 5. 12, 10, 9, 8, 13, 15;
6. 3, 6, 7, 0, 9, 4

**Page 83**
1. 19 – 10 = 9; 2. 18 – 10 = 8;
3. 17 – 10 = 7; 4. 18 – 10 = 8;
5. 19 – 10 = 9; 6. 17 – 10 = 7

**Page 84**
1. 0, 1, 2, 3, 4, 8, 7, 6, 8, 9, 10, 2, 1, 13; 2.
0, 13, 2, 3, 10, 9, 8, 7, 8, 9, 10, 3, 2, 13,
14; 3. 15, 1, 13, 3, 11, 5, 6, 8, 7, 6, 10, 11, 12,
2, 1, 15

**Page 85**
1. 0, 1, 2, 13, 12, 5, 6, 7, 8, 9, 6, 11, 4, 13, 2,
15, 0; 2. 0, 1, 15, 3, 13, 5, 6, 10, 8, 8, 10,
11, 12, 4, 14, 15, 16, 17; 3. 0, 17, 16, 15, 4, 5,
12, 11, 8, 9, 10, 11, 6, 5, 4, 15, 16, 1, 18

**Page 86**
1. +6; 2. –8; 3. +5; 4. +9;
5. –8; 6. –9

**Page 87**
1. 5 stripes; 2. 6 sand dollars; 3. 8
rings; 4. 7 drinks; 5. 8 seagulls; 6.
6 children

**Page 88**
True: 1. 15 – 7, 14 – 6, 18 – 10, 17 – 9; 2.
13 – 9, 12 – 8, 9 – 5; 3. 9 – 2, 11 – 4, 12
– 5, 15 – 8; 4. 8 – 6, 12 – 10, 9 – 7; 5.
14 – 9, 13 – 8, 11 – 6, 15 – 10; 6. 12 – 6,
15 – 9, 14 – 8

**Page 89**
Across: 1. fifteen; 2. sixteen; 3. twelve;
5. thirteen; 6. twenty; 7. eleven; 8.
nineteen; Down: 1. fourteen;
2. seventeen; 4. eighteen; 6. ten

**Page 90**
1. 86; 2. 49; 3. 58; 4. 56; 5. 45; 6. 91; 7.
92; 8. 65; 9. 34; 10. 62; 11. 67; 12. 84; 13.
13; 14. 21; 15. 30; 16. 76; 17. 103

**Page 91**
The numbers 1–50 should be written
on the lines. 50

**Page 92**
1. 54, 55, 56, 58, 60, 61, 63, 66, 67, 69;
2. 33, 35, 37, 39, 42, 44, 46, 48, 50; 3.
72, 73, 74, 78, 79, 81, 85, 86, 87, 90;
4. 101, 104, 106, 107, 110, 111, 113, 115, 116,
120

# Answer Key

**Page 93**
Before: 9, 5, 11, 20, 37, 13, 2, 66, 48, 7, 99; Between: 1, 26, 72, 20, 86, 50, 94, 100, 14, 59, 11; After: 91, 16, 30, 81, 19, 110, 40, 94, 22, 67, 16

**Page 94**
1. 1 ten, 6 ones; 2. 1 ten, 3 ones; 3. 1 ten, 9 ones; 4. 1 ten, 4 ones; 5. 1 ten, 5 ones; 6. 1 ten, 8 ones

**Page 95**
1. 43; 2. 57; 3. 46; 4. 62; 5. 34; 6. 95

**Page 96**
Check child's pictures.
1. 63; 2. 78; 3. 51; 4. 2; 5. 9; 6. 19

**Page 97**
1. 3 tens, 4 ones, 34; 2. 4 tens, 6 ones, 46; 3. 4 tens, 8 ones, 48; 4. 2 tens, 7 ones, 27; 5. 3 tens, 9 ones, 39; 6. 5 tens, 3 ones, 53

**Page 98**
1. 4, 14, 24, 34, 44, 54, 64, 74, 84, 94; 2. 70, 71, 72, 73, 74, 75, 76, 77, 78, 79; 3. 10, 20, 30, 40, 50, 60, 70, 80, 90, 100; 4. 1, 2, 3, 4, 5, 6, 7, 8, 9; 5. 60, 61, 62, 63, 64, 65, 66, 67, 68, 69; 6. 6, 16, 26, 36, 46, 56, 66, 76, 86, 96; 7. 7, 17, 27, 37, 47, 57, 67, 77, 87, 97; 8. 35

**Page 99**
1. 9 < 19; 2. 15 > 11; 3. 24 > 14; 4. 11 < 22; 5. 23 < 25; 6. 30 > 28; 7. 7 tens, 2 ones; 8. 9 tens, 6 ones; 9. 9 tens, 9 ones; 10. 8 tens, 4 ones; 11. 5 tens, 3 ones; 12. 4 tens, 7 ones

**Page 100**
1. <; 2. >; 3. >; 4. =; 5. >; 6. >; 7. <; 8. >; 9. <; 10. <

**Page 101**
1. 60, 60, 90, 70, 80; 2. 90, 70, 60, 80, 90; 3. 81, 64, 53, 46, 37; 4. Answers will vary.

**Page 102**
1. 40, 40, 30, 50, 10; 2. 40, 30, 10, 40, 20; 3. 46, 57, 74, 87, 28; 4. Answers will vary.

**Page 103**
1–4. Answers will vary.

**Page 104**
1. 1 ten, 2 ones; 2. 1 ten, 3 ones; 3. 1 ten, 8 ones; 4. 1 ten, 7 ones; 5. 22; 6. 21

**Page 105**
1. 72; 2. 81; 3. 31; 4. 72; 5. 41; 6. 55; 7. 32; 8. 22; 9. 50; 10. 60; 11. 44; 12. 58

**Page 106**
1. 1, 3, 2; 2. 3, 1, 2

**Page 107**
1. 6 units; 2. 5 units; 3. 9 units; 4. 3 units; 5. 8 units; 6. 6 units

**Page 108**
1. No. Answers will vary, but may include that the candies are different lengths. 2. Dawn, Sasha, Lynn; 3. Lucy, Answers will vary but may include that there are no gaps. 4. No. Answers will vary but may include the different lengths of their feet.

**Page 109**
1. 2:30; 2. 12:00; 3. 4:30; 4. 7:30; 5. 11:00; 6. 9:30

**Page 110**
1. A; 2. B; 3. A; 4. B; 5. C; 6. A

# Answer Key

**Page 111**
1. B; 2. D; 3. A; 4. C; 5. E

**Page 112**
1. 5 cows; 2. 8 pigs; 3. 5 – 4 = 1 more cow; 4. 8 – 4 = 4 fewer sheep; 5. 8 + 4 + 5 = 17 animals; 6. pigs

**Page 113**
1. 4 frogs; 2. Monday; 3. Wednesday; 4. 7 + 5 + 4 = 16 frogs; 5. Wednesday; 6. 7 – 5 = 2 more frogs

**Page 114**
1. 7 squares, 10 triangles, 3 rectangles; 2. 7 + 10 + 3 = 20; 3. 10 – 3 = 7; 4. 7 – 3 = 4; 5. the same number; 6. Answers will vary.

**Page 115**
triangle: 3 sides, 7 shapes; square: 4 sides, 6 shapes; rectangle: 4 sides, 4 shapes; circle: 0 sides, 8 shapes; trapezoid: 4 sides, 3 shapes

**Page 116**
Check child's drawings.
1. 4, 4, 4; 2. 0, 0, 0; 3. 3, 3, 3; 4. 4, 4, 4; 5. 4, 4, 4

**Page 117**
1. cone, cylinder; 2. cube, rectangular prism; 3. cone, cube; 4. 2 cylinders, cube; 5. cone, 2 cubes; 6. rectangular prism, 2 cubes

**Page 118**
1. not colored; 2. not colored; 3. colored; 4. colored; 5. not colored; 6. colored

**Page 119**
1. not colored; 2. colored; 3. colored; 4. not colored

**Page 120**
1. not colored; 2. colored; 3. not colored; 4. colored

**Page 121**
Answers will vary. Check child's drawings.

Which sentence has no mistakes?

A. Can you come over?

B. can you come over?

C. Can you come over.

Which sentence has no mistakes?

A. Maggie shared her book

B. maggie shared her book.

C. Maggie shared her book.

Name the picture. What is the vowel sound? Is it long or short?

Name the picture. What is the vowel sound? Is it long or short?

Which sentence has no mistakes?

A. Maggie shared her book

B. maggie shared her book.

(C.) Maggie shared her book.

Which sentence has no mistakes?

(A.) Can you come over?

B. can you come over?

C. Can you come over.

Name the picture. What is the vowel sound? Is it long or short?

## long a

Name the picture. What is the vowel sound? Is it long or short?

## short o

## Name the picture. What is the vowel sound? Is it long or short?

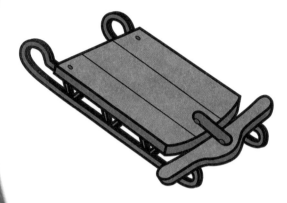

## Name the picture. What is the vowel sound? Is it long or short?

## Name the picture. What is the vowel sound? Is it long or short?

## Which letters spell the last sound of the word?

**S O ___ ___**

# Name the picture. What is the vowel sound? Is it long or short?

## long e

# Name the picture. What is the vowel sound? Is it long or short?

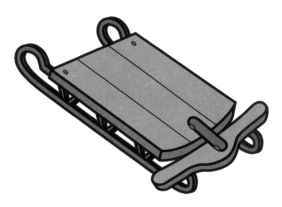

## short e

# Which letters spell the last sound of the word?

## s o _c_ _k_

# Name the picture. What is the vowel sound? Is it long or short?

## long o

## Which letters spell the first sound of the word?

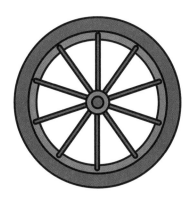

__ __ e e l

## Which letters spell the long vowel sound?

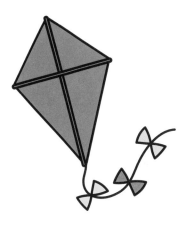

k __ t __

## Which letters spell the long vowel sound?

l __ __ f

## Name the picture. How many vowel sounds does it have? How many syllables does it have?

## Which letters spell the long vowel sound?

**k _i_ t _e_**

## Which letters spell the first sound of the word?

_w_ _h_ **e e l**

## Name the picture. How many vowel sounds does it have? How many syllables does it have?

The word *sandwich* has two vowel sounds and two syllables.

## Which letters spell the long vowel sound?

**l _e_ _a_ f**

Name the picture.
How many vowel
sounds does it have?
How many syllables
does it have?

Read the sentence.
Which word is a
common noun?

Sam played at
the park.

Read the sentence.
Which word is a
proper noun?

My friend moved
to Utah.

Which pronoun
could take the place
of the underlined
words?

Mrs. Shay
watered the
flowers in <u>Mrs.
Shay's</u> yard.

Language Arts
L.1.1b

**Read the sentence. Which word is a common noun?**

**Sam played at the park.**

Language Arts
RF.1.3d

**Name the picture. How many vowel sounds does it have? How many syllables does it have?**

The word *banana* has three vowel sounds and three syllables.

Language Arts
L.1.1d

**Which pronoun could take the place of the underlined words?**

**Mrs. Shay watered the flowers in her yard.**

Language Arts
L.1.1b

**Read the sentence. Which word is a proper noun?**

**My friend moved to Utah.**

Which pronoun could take the place of the underlined words?

Nate will listen to any ideas you tell <u>Nate</u>.

Choose the verb that tells what happened in the past.

She (saw, sees) the movie last week.

Choose the verb that tells what is happening now.

The puppet makes the baby (will laugh, laugh).

Choose the verb that tells what will happen in the future.

My cousin (visited, will visit) in June.

Choose the verb that tells what happened in the past.

She (saw, sees) the movie last week.

Which pronoun could take the place of the underlined words?

Nate will listen to any ideas you tell him.

Choose the verb that tells what will happen in the future.

My cousin (visited, will visit) in June.

Choose the verb that tells what is happening now.

The puppet makes the baby (will laugh, laugh).

Read the sentence. Which word is an adjective?

The koala had soft fur.

Read the sentence. Which word is an adjective?

Three children live next door.

Read the sentence. Which word is a conjunction?

Marc and Tia shared the swing.

Read the sentence. Which word is a conjunction?

I like peas, but I don't like carrots.

Read the sentence. Which word is an adjective?

Three children live next door.

Read the sentence. Which word is an adjective?

The koala had soft fur.

Read the sentence. Which word is a conjunction?

I like peas, but I don't like carrots.

Read the sentence. Which word is a conjunction?

Marc and Tia shared the swing.

Which word is not a conjunction?

A. so

B. and

C. but

D. ever

Choose a word to complete the sentence.

We will take (a, an) airplane to Florida.

Choose a word to complete the sentence.

I want to play on (a, an) baseball team.

Read the sentence. Which word is a preposition?

Did you look under the chair?

Choose a word to complete the sentence.

We will take (a, (an)) airplane to Florida.

Which word is not a conjunction?

A. so

B. and

C. but

(D.) ever

Read the sentence. Which word is a preposition?

Did you look under the chair?

Choose a word to complete the sentence.

I want to play on (a,) an) baseball team.

Read the sentence. Which word is a preposition?

Let's walk toward the pond.

Which word is not a preposition?

A. during

B. sit

C. after

D. around

Which is a telling sentence?

A. Hand me the cup.

B. I like the blue cup.

C. Do you have a cup?

D. The cup spilled!

Which sentence shows strong feeling?

A. The game is later today.

B. We won the game!

C. What time does the game start?

D. Don't forget the game.

Which word is not a preposition?

A. during

B. sit

C. after

D. around

Read the sentence. Which word is a preposition?

Let's walk toward the pond.

Which sentence shows strong feeling?

A. The game is later today.

B. We won the game!

C. What time does the game start?

D. Don't forget the game.

Which is a telling sentence?

A. Hand me the cup.

B. I like the blue cup.

C. Do you have a cup?

D. The cup spilled!

Which is an asking sentence?

A. Be careful with the hot soup.

B. Watch out for the hot soup!

C. Is the soup too hot?

D. This soup has green beans.

Which sentence gives a command?

A. This is our fort.

B. Climb in carefully.

C. Do you like it?

D. We built it in one day!

Read the sentence. Which word should begin with a capital letter?

Ann and suki came to my party.

Read the sentence. Which word should begin with a capital letter?

Amelia jones is my best friend.

**Which sentence gives a command?**

A. This is our fort.

(B.) Climb in carefully.

C. Do you like it?

D. We built it in one day!

**Which is an asking sentence?**

A. Be careful with the hot soup.

B. Watch out for the hot soup!

(C.) Is the soup too hot?

D. This soup has green beans.

**Read the sentence. Which word should begin with a capital letter?**

**Amelia Jones is my best friend.**

**Read the sentence. Which word should begin with a capital letter?**

**Ann and Suki came to my party.**

Which date is correct?

A. monday, april 16

B. June 15, 2015

C. december 4

Which date is missing a capital letter?

A. May 23, 2013

B. Wednesday, June 22

C. Friday, april 10

Which punctuation mark belongs at the end of the sentence?

.   ?   !

Watch out

Which punctuation mark belongs at the end of the sentence?

.   ?   !

The sun is setting

Which date is missing a capital letter?

A. May 23, 2013

B. Wednesday, June 22

C. Friday, april 10

Which date is correct?

A. monday, april 16

B. June 15, 2015

C. december 4

Which punctuation mark belongs at the end of the sentence?

. ? !

The sun is setting

Which punctuation mark belongs at the end of the sentence?

. ? !

Watch out

Which punctuation mark belongs at the end of the sentence?

.   ?   !

When did the baby wake up

Which date is correct?

A. November 11 2016

B. August 30, 2015

C. January 25 1997

Which date is missing a comma?

A. June 19, 2015

B. September 8 2016

C. October 22, 1952

Which boxes should contain commas?

We played☐ *Go Fish*☐ *Old Maid*☐ and *War*.

Which date is
correct?

A. November 11
2016

(B.) August 30,
2015

C. January 25
1997

Which punctuation
mark belongs at the
end of the sentence?

. (?) !

When did the
baby wake up

Which boxes should
contain commas?

We played□ *Go
Fish*□ *Old Maid*□
and *War*.

Which date is
missing a comma?

A. June 19, 2015

(B.) September 8
2016

C. October 22,
1952

## Which boxes should contain commas?

## Bring your pillow☐ sleeping☐ bag☐ and pajamas.

## Which word is misspelled?

## A. enuff

## B. group

## C. eyes

## Which word is misspelled?

## A. ready

## B. hav

## C. many

## Which word is misspelled?

## A. through

## B. some

## C. earlee

Which word is misspelled?

A. enough

B. group

C. eyes

Which boxes should contain commas?

Bring your pillow☐ sleeping☐ bag☐ and pajamas.

Which word is misspelled?

A. through

B. some

C. early

Which word is misspelled?

A. ready

B. have

C. many

Which word is misspelled?

A. sayed

B. again

C. either

What does the underlined word mean?

After its bath, the dog's fur was <u>soggy</u>.

What does the underlined word mean?

In fall, the tree <u>sheds</u> its leaves.

What does the underlined word mean?

The baby was <u>glum</u> after she lost her toy.

What does the underlined word mean?

After its bath, the dog's fur was <u>soggy</u>.

wet

Which word is misspelled?

A. said

B. again

C. either

What does the underlined word mean?

The baby was <u>glum</u> after she lost her toy.

sad

What does the underlined word mean?

In fall, the tree <u>sheds</u> its leaves.

drops

Which word means "do again"?

A. doing

B. redo

C. undo

Which word means "more than one dream"?

A. dreaming

B. dreamed

C. dreams

What is the root word for all these words?

napped

napping

naps

What is the root word for all these words?

unlock

locks

locking

**Which word means "more than one dream"?**

A. dreaming

B. dreamed

**C. dreams**

**Which word means "do again"?**

A. doing

**B. redo**

C. undo

**What is the root word for all these words?**

unlock

locks

locking

lock

**What is the root word for all these words?**

napped

napping

naps

nap

Which has the root word *heat*?

A. hot

B. reheat

C. eat

Which has the root word *cry*?

A. unhappy

B. crying

C. dry

Which is furry?

A. robin

B. rabbit

C. grasshopper

Which is creamy?

A. broccoli

B. cracker

C. milk

Which has the root word *cry*?

A. unhappy

(B.) crying

C. dry

Which has the root word *heat*?

A. hot

(B.) reheat

C. eat

Which is creamy?

A. broccoli

B. cracker

(C.) milk

Which is furry?

A. robin

(B.) rabbit

C. grasshopper

Which would you use
for cooking?

A. wrench

B. sponge

C. whisk

Which would you use
for painting?

A. smock

B. rake

C. wire

Spilling a cup of
water is

A. tragic.

B. unfortunate.

C. disastrous.

One grain of sand is

A. small.

B. undersized.

C. tiny.

## Which would you use for painting?

**(A.) smock**

**B. rake**

**C. wire**

## Which would you use for cooking?

**A. wrench**

**B. sponge**

**(C.) whisk**

## One grain of sand is

**A. small.**

**B. undersized.**

**(C.) tiny.**

## Spilling a cup of water is

**A. tragic.**

**(B.) unfortunate.**

**C. disastrous.**

One loaf of bread had 8 slices. Another loaf had 9 slices. How many slices of bread were there in all?

Jake has a puzzle with 20 pieces. Seven pieces fell on the floor. How many pieces are not on the floor?

The Storm soccer team scored 3 goals on Monday and 6 goals on Saturday. How many goals did they score this week?

The Jones family bought a dozen muffins and ate nine of them. How many muffins were left?

Jake has a puzzle with 20 pieces. Seven pieces fell on the floor. How many pieces are not on the floor?

## 13 puzzle pieces

One loaf of bread had 8 slices. Another loaf had 9 slices. How many slices of bread were there in all?

## 17 slices

The Jones family bought a dozen muffins and ate nine of them. How many muffins were left?

## 3 muffins

The Storm soccer team scored 3 goals on Monday and 6 goals on Saturday. How many goals did they score this week?

## 9 goals

A toy car raced for 12 seconds. Then, it raced for 8 seconds. How many seconds did it race in all?

Ezra had 10 kittens in his lap. Four kittens crawled off. How many kittens were left?

Count the groups of dots. How many in all?

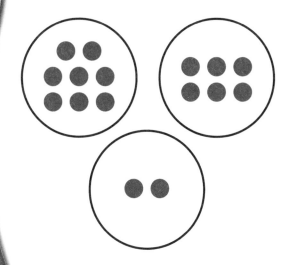

Count the groups of dots. How many in all?

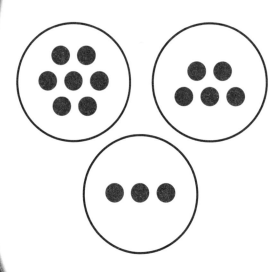

**Math**
1.OA.A.1

**Ezra had 10 kittens in his lap. Four kittens crawled off. How many kittens were left?**

## 6 kittens

**Math**
1.OA.A.1

**A toy car raced for 12 seconds. Then, it raced for 8 seconds. How many seconds did it race in all?**

## 20 seconds

**Math**
1.OA.A.2

**Count the groups of dots. How many in all?**

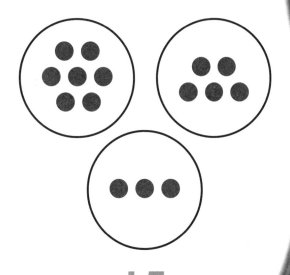

## 15

**Math**
1.OA.A.2

**Count the groups of dots. How many in all?**

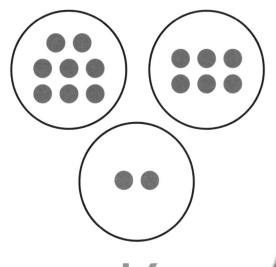

## 16

## Which pair is true?

$8 + 3 = 11$

$3 + 11 = 8$

$7 + 6 = 13$

$6 + 7 = 13$

## Which pair is true?

$12 + 4 = 16$

$4 + 12 = 16$

$8 + 9 = 18$

$9 + 8 = 18$

## Which is true?

$8 + 8 + 2 = 8 + 10$

$4 + 9 + 2 = 4 + 10$

## Which is true?

$1 + 7 + 9 = 17 + 9$

$6 + 4 + 3 = 10 + 3$

## Which pair is true?

12 + 4 = 16
4 + 12 = 16

8 + 9 = 18
9 + 8 = 18

## Which pair is true?

8 + 3 = 11
3 + 11 = 8

7 + 6 = 13
6 + 7 = 13

## Which is true?

1 + 7 + 9 = 17 + 9

6 + 4 + 3 = 10 + 3

## Which is true?

8 + 8 + 2 = 8 + 10

4 + 9 + 2 = 4 + 10

## Which helps you find the answer to 10 – 6?

A. $8 + 2 = 10$

B. $6 + 4 = 10$

C. $10 - 3 = 7$

## Which helps you find the answer to 18 – 7?

A. $17 - 5 = 12$

B. $9 + 9 = 18$

C. $7 + 11 = 18$

## What number makes 10 when added to 7?

## Which is the same as 9 + 6?

A. $9 + 1 + 6 =$
   $10 + 6 = 16$

B. $9 + 1 + 5 =$
   $10 + 5 = 15$

**Which helps you find the answer to 18 – 7?**

A. 17 – 5 = 12

B. 9 + 9 = 18

**C.** 7 + 11 = 18

**Which helps you find the answer to 10 – 6?**

A. 8 + 2 = 10

**B.** 6 + 4 = 10

C. 10 – 3 = 7

**Which is the same as 9 + 6?**

A. 9 + 1 + 6 = 10 + 6 = 16

**B.** 9 + 1 + 5 = 10 + 5 = 15

**What number makes 10 when added to 7?**

3

Which is the same as
8 + 7?

A. 10 + 5

B. 10 – 5

C. 10 + 4

Which is the same as
15 – 6?

A. 15 – 10 – 2

B. 15 – 5 – 1

C. 15 + 6

Which is the same as
11 – 8?

A. 11 – 5 – 4

B. 10 – 8

C. 10 – 7

Complete the fact
family.

12 + 7 = 19

7 + 12 = 19

19 – 7 = 12

☐ – ☐ = ☐

## Which is the same as 15 – 6?

A. 15 – 10 – 2

B. 15 – 5 – 1

C. 15 + 6

## Which is the same as 8 + 7?

A. 10 + 5

B. 10 – 5

C. 10 + 4

## Complete the fact family.

12 + 7 = 19

7 + 12 = 19

19 – 7 = 12

19 – 12 = 7

## Which is the same as 11 – 8?

A. 11 – 5 – 4

B. 10 – 8

C. 10 – 7

## Complete the fact family.

$13 + 4 = 17$

$\boxed{\phantom{00}} + \boxed{\phantom{00}} = \boxed{\phantom{00}}$

$17 - 4 = 13$

$17 - 13 = 4$

## Which is the same as 8 + 9?

A. $9 + 8 + 1$

B. $10 + 10$

C. $8 + 8 + 1$

## Which is the same as 6 + 9?

A. $6 + 6 + 3$

B. $5 + 11$

C. $6 + 8 + 5$

## Which equation is false?

A. $5 + 3 = 4 + 4$

B. $16 + 4 = 10 + 9$

C. $13 - 4 = 11 - 2$

## Which is the same as 8 + 9?

A. $9 + 8 + 1$

B. $10 + 10$

C. $8 + 8 + 1$

## Complete the fact family.

$13 + 4 = 17$

$\boxed{4} + \boxed{13} = \boxed{17}$

$17 - 4 = 13$

$17 - 13 = 4$

## Which equation is false?

A. $5 + 3 = 4 + 4$

B. $16 + 4 = 10 + 9$

C. $13 - 4 = 11 - 2$

## Which is the same as 6 + 9?

A. $6 + 6 + 3$

B. $5 + 11$

C. $6 + 8 + 5$

## Which equation is true?

A. $14 - 6 = 12 - 4$

B. $11 + 4 = 9 + 5$

C. $14 + 3 = 8 + 8$

## What number makes the equation true?

$12 = \boxed{\phantom{00}} - 4$

## What number makes the equation true?

$11 + \boxed{\phantom{00}} = 17$

## What number has 1 ten and 5 ones?

## What number makes the equation true?

$$12 = \boxed{16} - 4$$

## Which equation is true?

**A.** $14 - 6 = 12 - 4$

**B.** $11 + 4 = 9 + 5$

**C.** $14 + 3 = 8 + 8$

## What number has 1 ten and 5 ones?

15

## What number makes the equation true?

$$11 + \boxed{6} = 17$$

# What number has 1 ten and 2 ones?

# What number has 6 tens and 0 ones?

# What number has 3 tens and 0 ones?

# Compare.

41 ◯ 14

## What number has 6 tens and 0 ones?

60

## What number has 1 ten and 2 ones?

12

## Compare.

41 ⊘ 14

## What number has 3 tens and 0 ones?

30

Compare.

**96** ◯ **69**

Compare.

**38** ◯ **83**

Compare.

**25** ◯ **52**

$$\begin{array}{r} 42 \\ +\ 7 \\ \hline \end{array}$$

## Compare.

38 (<) 83

## Compare.

96  69

$$
\begin{array}{r}
42 \\
+\ 7 \\
\hline
49
\end{array}
$$

## Compare.

25 (<) 52

68
+ 3

26
+ 20

38
+ 30

## What number is ten more than 89?

$$\begin{array}{r} 26 \\ +\ 20 \\ \hline 46 \end{array}$$

$$\begin{array}{r} 68 \\ +\ 3 \\ \hline 71 \end{array}$$

## What number is ten more than 89?

99

$$\begin{array}{r} 38 \\ +\ 30 \\ \hline 68 \end{array}$$

# What number is ten more than 42?

# What number is ten less than 87?

$$80 - 20$$

$$70 - 30$$

## What number is ten less than 87?

77

## What number is ten more than 42?

52

$$70 - 30 = 40$$

$$80 - 20 = 60$$

$$\begin{array}{r} 90 \\ -\ 80 \\ \hline \end{array}$$

# How many units long is the banana?

# How many units long is the caterpillar?

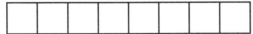

# What time is shown?

## How many units long is the banana?

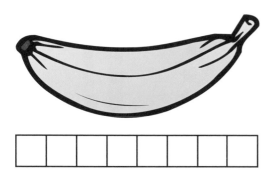

**8 units**

$$90 - 80 = 10$$

## What time is shown?

**8:00**

## How many units long is the caterpillar?

**4 units**

# What time is shown?

# What time is shown?

# What time is shown?

# What time is shown?

# What time is shown?

# 12:00

# What time is shown?

# 2:00

# What time is shown?

# 1:30

# What time is shown?

# 4:30

## What time is shown?

## At the park, Mel saw 4 dogs, 8 squirrels, and 12 birds. How many of the animals had four legs?

## A cafeteria served 12 cups of orange juice, 6 cups of apple juice, and 10 cups of milk. How many cups of fruit juice were served?

## Which shapes have four sides?

At the park, Mel saw 4 dogs, 8 squirrels, and 12 birds. How many of the animals had four legs?

12

What time is shown?

10:30

Which shapes have four sides?

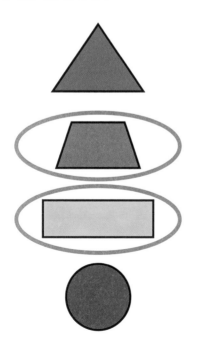

A cafeteria served 12 cups of orange juice, 6 cups of apple juice, and 10 cups of milk. How many cups of fruit juice were served?

18

# Which shape has three corners?

# Which shape has no corners?

# Which shows one half?

# Which shows three quarters?

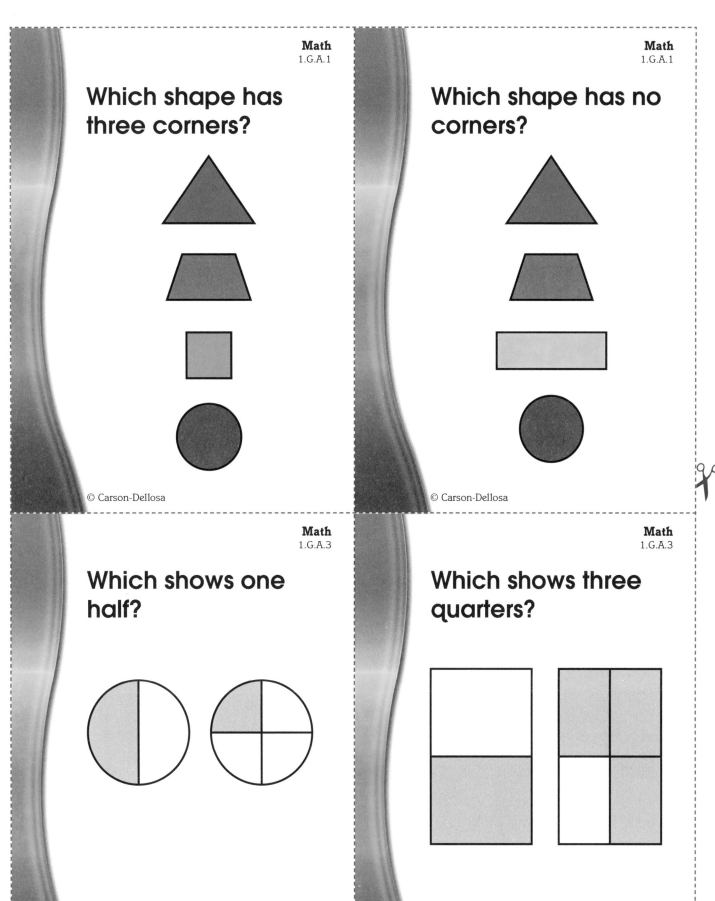

# Which shape has no corners?

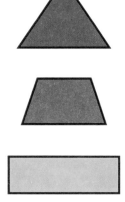

# Which shape has three corners?

# Which shows three quarters?

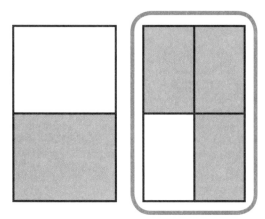

# Which shows one half?

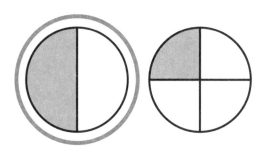

# Which shows one fourth?

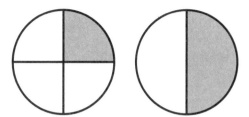

# Which shows two fourths?

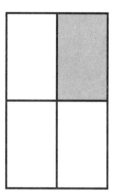 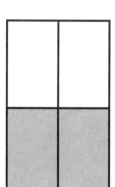

# Which shows one whole?

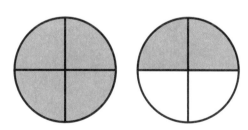

# Which shows one whole?

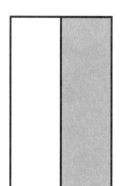 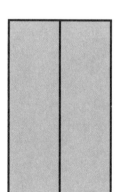

**Math**
1.G.A.3

# Which shows two fourths?

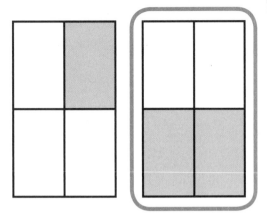

**Math**
1.G.A.3

# Which shows one fourth?

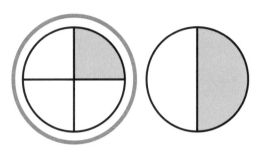

**Math**
1.G.A.3

# Which shows one whole?

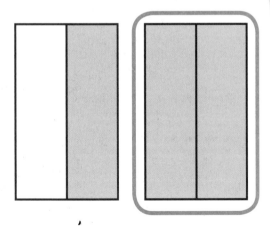

**Math**
1.G.A.3

# Which shows one whole?

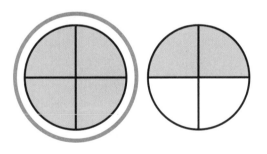